Beat for Peace is a collaborative intervention that combines the best school counseling practices. A truly unique convergence occurs when beliefs of a professional school counselor into a world music drum ensemble. Once the hand strikes the drum the accessibility and power of the drum becomes apparent.

The lessons in this book are designed to enhance the fun of drumming with the spoken word, and therapeutic ear. Everything is research based and has been utilized in my own Beat for Peace ensemble since 1999. Each lesson is included for a specific purpose and with desired student outcomes in mind. Every year, my desired student outcomes are adapted to meet the needs of my Title I school population. I encourage you to do the same. Take these lessons and implement them as written in the order provided, or make them your own by expanding the content or adjusting the sequence. The important thing is to tailor your drum ensemble intervention to the needs of your target population.

Towards the end of the book, you will find a parent education component. We all understand the demands on our students' families and often go to great lengths to make our school building accessible, attractive, and welcoming. These six lessons do just that. Families can relate to drumming. I can't think of a single concert in which we did not had family members approach to comment on a song that reminded them of "old nursery rhyme" or "a song my mama used to sing to me". Many times a spontaneous jam broke out as we concluded the night. Try the parent lessons out. Not only will they enjoy drumming, they'll also learn about effective communication, encouraging responsibility and stress management.

At the heart of it all, Beat for Peace is an intervention designed to help kids learn, feel confident in their abilities, and to develop the attitudes, skills and beliefs of a resilient person. As you implement these lessons make sure that you are practicing within your own areas of expertise. Your work must be consistent with your state department of education's professional standards and ethical codes of conduct. If at any time you become concerned about your performance or the responses of a student, I encourage you to seek out consultation or assistance from other school counselors, your administrator or school district staff.

Finally, my deepest gratitude is extended to Paul Corbiere, my colleague and co-founder of Beat for Peace. He brought drumming into my personal and professional life. I am grateful Will Schmid, author of <u>World Music Drumming: A Cross Cultural Curriculum</u>, which is the backbone of the intervention. I welcome the support of Susan Saint John, Principal for having the confidence to allow drum circles to happen in her school. I celebrate with the school counselors, music educators, mental health professionals, school teachers, social workers, grief therapists, community activist and students who have shared in my drumming journey. I am humored, encouraged and embraced by my loving and supportive family; Debbie, Paul, and Savannah. Thanks for letting me have the time to write the book. Love you guys!

I hope you enjoy the book. I sure enjoyed writing it!

Peace,

Mike

This page intentionally left blank.

Table of Contents

The Beat for Peace Model	**9**
Tips on Running a successful Beat for Peace Intervention	**13**
Dunno: The Talking Drum Small Group Counseling	**21**
The Beat for Peace Model: Listen-Focus-Respect	**27**
The Research of Beat for Peace	**31**
Why Beat for Peace	**35**
Dunno: The Talking Drums Lessons	**39**
Lesson 1 – Welcome Session	41
Lesson 2 – Hello Bongo	43
Lesson 3 – Drum Compact	47
Lesson 4 – Decorate Your Drum	53
Lesson 5 – Student PreSurvey	57
Lesson 6 – The Powerful Positive Attitude	59
Lesson 7 – Hopes and Dreams	65
Lesson 8 – Goal Setting	71
Lesson 9 – Communication Skills	83
Lesson 10 – Relationships-Friendship Skills	97
Lesson 11 – Solving Peer Pressure Problems	101
Lesson 12 – Future Planning	109
Lesson 13 – Moving On	117

Beat for Peace Family: Drumming and Parent Education — 119

Parent Lesson 1 – Listening Skills in the Family	123
Parent Lesson 2 – Communication and I-Messages in the Family	129
Parent Lesson 3 – Responsibility in the Family	135
Parent Lesson 4 – Teamwork in the Family	139
Parent Lesson 5 – Listen, Focus and Respect in the Family	141
Parent Lesson 6 – Balance in the Family	145

Forms and Tools — 147

Drum Ensemble Student Referral Form	149
Drum Ensemble Permission Slip	153
Drum Ensemble Compact	157
Hello Bongo!	161
Student Pre-Survey	165
Student Post-Survey	169
Teacher Rating Scale	173
Weekly Check-In Sheet	177
Drummer Self-Evaluation Report	181
Guided Interview: Parent Version / Teacher Version	185

Research and References — 189

The Beat for Peace Model

Listen-Focus-Respect

This page intentionally left blank.

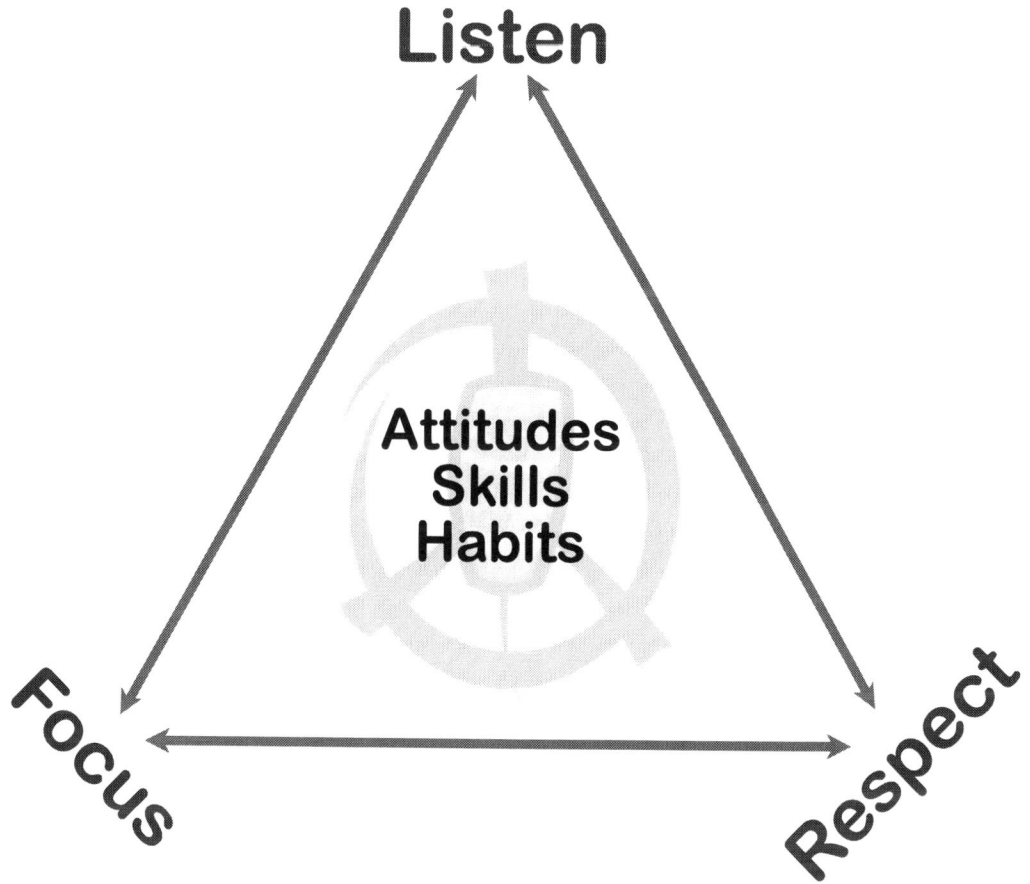

The 6 Keys

1. **LISTEN-FOCUS-RESPECT** are interconnected.
2. **LISTEN-FOCUS-RESPECT** leads to academic success.
3. **LISTEN-FOCUS-RESPECT** leads to successful relationships with families, peers, teachers and authority figures.
4. **LISTEN-FOCUS-RESPECT** leads to college and career readiness.
5. **LISTEN-FOCUS-RESPECT** can be modeled, taught, and encouraged.
6. Students come to us with different attitudes, levels of skill, and a mixture of good and bad habits. We can improve the ability of students to **LISTEN-FOCUS-RESPECT**.

This page intentionally left blank.

Tips on Running a Successful Beat for Peace Intervention

This page intentionally left blank.

Tips on Running a Successful Beat for Peace Intervention

- What is a drum ensemble? How is it different than a drum circle?

- What is the role of the drum ensemble leader/facilitator?

- Ten things to remember when leading a drum ensemble.
    1. Show, don't tell.
    2. Don't be afraid to repeat something until it is right.
    3. Faster is not always better.
    4. Everyone has their own part to play – it's not music until we put it all together, shake it up (rotate parts).
    5. If you can sing it - you can play it.
    6. Drum to dance – dance to sing – sing to drum.
    7. Have fun.
    8. Master it before you try to teach it.
    9. Approach the drum as if this might be the last time you get to play it.
    10. Have an established attention signal (call-response).

- What is the Talking Drum? Why meet with students outside of the drum ensemble?

- What is the value of data (process and outcome)?

- Tips for recruiting students and involving teachers.

- The icing on the cake: websites, recognition, shirts, photos, cd's.

- Beat for Peace, **Represent.**

- It's about meaningful connections and high expectations. Conduct research on resiliency and efficacy.

What is a drum ensemble? How is it different than a drum circle?

I developed a definition for drum ensemble after years of playing in one and with the help my drummer buddies. I view a drum ensemble as a group that has an identified leader who teaches the culture of drumming, how to drum, and drumming songs. The songs have specific parts (timeline, high drum, medium drum, etc) and the members of the drum ensemble are responsible for their part. I view a drum circle as a less structured group in which there is a facilitator who guides the music but doesn't lead or teach as in an ensemble.

Beat for Peace is a drum ensemble. We have a leader. We learn songs, often with roots in West Africa and the Caribbean. The students have their specific parts in the song. When we bring it all together, we produce music.

What is the role of the drum ensemble leader?

The job of the drum ensemble leader is to teach the students how to drum, teach the key concepts of a successful drum ensemble (see World Music Drumming: A Cross Cultural Curriculum), teach the music, expose the students to the culture and history of drumming, and to develop the attitudes, skills and behaviors of Listen-Focus-Respect.

10 things to remember when leading a drum ensemble.

1. Show, don't tell
    - DON'T OVER-TALK. Drumming is taught using echo patterns, call-response, and question answer. Show the students the part. Sing the part then play the part. Model Listen-Focus-Respect. Communicate your directions using non-verbals and body language.

2. Don't be afraid to repeat something until it is right
    - Yes, we all want to start and finish an ensemble so that we can jam! Avoid the temptation. Drumming is not an "immediate gratification" activity. Stick on a rhythm, timeline or portion of the ensemble until everyone has it correct. Develop teamwork by encouraging your drummers to help those around him/her. Get the foundation solid before you move on or your ensemble will crumble.

3. Faster is not always better
    - This was taught to me my second year of drumming. I had learned my part in the ensemble on which we were working and wanted to crank it up a notch. Others were not ready and since the ensemble wasn't just about *me*, the leader told me that faster was not faster. In other words, be patient. The goal is to play cleanly and correctly, not sloppy and fast.

4. Shake it up!
   - Rotate parts. Try not to let your students play the same drum all year long. When learning an ensemble, have everyone stand up and shift parts. It not only keeps it interesting for the students, it is developing depth in your drum ensemble. When students can play multiple parts, they can cover multiple parts. Learning all the parts increases understanding of how the various rhythms fit into the timeline.

5. If you can sing it - you can play it
   - Get out your singing voice. I know it's scary, but do it anyway. Have your drummers sing their parts before they touch the drums. Sing it first. Play it second.

6. Drum to dance – dance to sing – sing to drum
   - There is an old saying that goes something like "drum to dance, dance to sing, sing to drum." I probably misquoted the saying, but the true meaning is obvious. Drumming, dancing and singing go together. Most ensembles have lyrics to sing and dance moves to make. Expand your group's comfort level and repertoire to include singing and dancing.

7. Have fun
   - Seems simple. Leading a drum ensemble can be challenging and stressful. Relax! Make it fun. Laugh at your mistakes and spread joy with your successes. Have fun. Balance fun with respect.

8. Master it before you try to teach it
   - Make sure you master an ensemble before you present it to your students. Don't get halfway though teaching the parts only to find yourself stuck with the low drum part. Take the time to learn all of the parts and to figure out where they fall along the timeline.

9. Approach the drum as if this might be the last time you get to play it
   - Every year we have one or more of our students move or leave the drum ensemble unexpectedly. Sometimes that departure is forced by the distressing realities of their families and lives. Talk to your students about what it means to play like it's the last time they will be able to play. Give each rehearsal and performance 100% effort, 100% focus and 100% respect.

10. Have an established attention signal (call-response)
    - We use *ago-ame*. You can use whatever you want. The important thing is to establish a call and response in which the response is to freeze, look at the adult, and stop talking. The call is given when you need to give instructions, manage behavior or to otherwise get the group back on track. Teach and practice the call and response frequently.

What is the Talking Drum? Why meet with students outside of the drum ensemble?

The Talking Drum or DUNNO is the group that meets with the school counselor outside of the ensemble rehearsals. DUNNO sessions are based on the lessons included in this curriculum and are conducted in manner consistent with best practices of classroom guidance lessons. DUNNO sessions reinforce and expand on those teachings that were initiated in the drum ensemble rehearsal. We found that students wanted and needed more help with communication, goal setting, and positive attitude management and so on. DUNNO sessions give this opportunity

What is the value of data (process and outcome)?

Data is your friend. Say it, "Data is my friend." Beat for Peace is an intervention that is designed to produce specific student outcomes such as academic gains, behavioral gains, improved attendance, and improved self-efficacy. Become friends with your school's data warehouse manager and collect objective data elements what will help you document role in support student achievement. Teacher, parent and student surveys provide for process data that gives a "face" to the intervention. Remember, data is your friend.

Tips for recruiting students and involving teachers.

The *Beat for Peace Student Referral Form* (available in the Forms and Tools section) is the first step in selecting student drummers. Students should be selected based on academic, behavioral, or esteem related need. How do you know who needs the intervention? ASK YOUR TEACHERS. Reach out to your teachers and ask "Who do you need help with?" Offer to work with the students who drive the teachers nuts. It helps the student. It also helps the teacher. Once you have student recruits, keep your teachers in the loop by asking them how your student drummers are behaving in the classrooms. The *Weekly Report* and *Teacher Survey* are effective communication tools. Take steps to hold the student accountable for their behavior outside of the drum circle. Do this and your staff will see you and a resource and your program as a benefit to the school.

The icing on the cake: website, recognition, shirts, photos, cd's.

In the presence of caring and supportive adults, students feel connected to the school and the drum ensemble group. Create a group identity by having a logo design, drum ensemble shirts, a website, and plenty of photographs. Fundraise, right a grant, or seek out benefactors – do whatever it takes to provide you students with these tangible trappings of affiliation.

Beat for Peace, *Represent.*

When my drum ensemble goes anywhere, we represent. That means we are "performing" anytime we are wearing our logo t-shirt. We represent the group and our school well by behaving with Focus and Respect. Student drummers should represent the drum ensemble by practicing **Listen-Focus-Respect** in the classroom, at lunch, in the hallway, on stage and at all times. We speak about how one person can make the group look good or look bad based on his or her actions.

> It's about meaningful connections and high expectations. Seek out research on resiliency and efficacy.

Beat for Peace, founded by Mike Kane and Paul Corbiere, is based on research put forth in the resiliency literature. People with resiliency are said to be able to bounce back from life's stressors, to be successful in spite of adversity. By providing caring and support, high expectations, and opportunities for meaningful participation Beat for Peace is able to build the characteristics of resiliency in children.

Research shows the characteristics of resilient students to be similar to those key concepts being taught by the World Music Drumming: A Cross Cultural Curriculum. We monopolized on this complementary relationship and have been successful in helping students exposed to various intrinsic and extrinsic risk factors.

Student Self- Efficacy is defined as the student's belief that he or she can learn. Teacher self-efficacy is defined as the teacher's belief that he/she can teach a student and his/her belief that the student can be taught. In other words, an efficacious student believes that he/she can learn and the efficacious teacher believes that he/she can teach. The students selected for Beat for Peace are often stuck in a disabling feedback loop. They have a history of negative messages about their academic or behavioral proficiency. Through Beat for Peace we seek to flip the feedback loop to a more positive sequence in which students are recognized for their incremental gains towards a meaningful proficiency target. We are retraining the mind from negative attitudes to positive attitudes through efficacious interventions.

This page intentionally left blank.

DUNNO

The Talking Drum Themes

This page intentionally left blank.

DUNNO Small Group Counseling Sessions

- Listen, Focus, Respect
- Positive Attitude Management
- Multiple Intelligences, Learning Styles
- Goal Setting (Academic & Behavioral)
- Effective Communication
- Friendship Skills
- Peer Refusal Skills
- Aspirations: College and Career Readiness

Photo Credit: Ann Newmann

Beat for Peace
DUNNO Themes

MONTH	KEY ATTITUDE, SKILL, AND HABIT	TOPIC	ACTIVITIES
September/ October	Listen Focus Respect	Introduction, Rules, Rapport Building Listen-Focus-Respect	**Introduce:** Decorate Your Drum sheet. **Discuss:** "A Circle is a symbol of equality – Within it we shall find respect" **Forms:** Decorate Your Drum, Drum Compact, Student Survey (Pre-Test), and Teacher Rating
November	Respect	Positive Attitude / Optimism	**Review:** Listen, Focus, Respect **Introduce:** Stop-Think-Choose **Discuss:** Positive attitude, management of one's own attitude, and self-talk.
December/January	Focus	Developing Hopes & Dreams Academic Goal Setting	**Review:** Positive Attitude **Introduce:** Hopes, Dreams, Goal Setting **Discuss:** Sense of purpose and future, goal setting steps, self-efficacy. **Forms:** Teacher Rating, Report Card Grades, and Assessment Data

MONTH	KEY ATTITUDE, SKILL, AND HABIT	TOPIC	ACTIVITIES
February/March	Listen Focus Respect	Communication	**Review:** Goal Setting, Monitor Progress **Introduce:** Communication, Listening, Speaking and Empathy Discuss: Communication skills in a variety of social situations. Stress the importance of effective communication with adults. Emphasize how drum circle skills and techniques apply to verbal communication. **Forms:** Drummer Self-Evaluation
April	Respect	Relationships	**Review:** Communication, Listening, Speaking, Empathy and Monitor Goal Progress **Discuss:** Define the qualities of healthy relationships. Define the attitudes, skills and behaviors of a good friend. Learn and practice I-Messages.
May	Focus Respect	Peer Pressure	**Review:** Qualities of healthy relationships **Introduce:** Peer Pressure, Peer Pressure Refusal Strategies Discuss: Positive and negative aspects of peer pressure. Stress the importance of effective refusal strategies to avoid destructive decisions.

MONTH	KEY ATTITUDE, SKILL, AND HABIT	TOPIC	ACTIVITIES
May	Listen Focus Respect	Future Planning Moving On Ceremony	**Review:** Listen, Focus, Respect **Discuss:** SCANS skills, career success, student experiences that occurred inside and outside of the drum ensemble. Offer celebrations for the group's successes. **Forms:** Student Post Survey, Teacher Rating Scale, Certificates.

The Beat for Peace Model

Listen-Focus-Respect

This page intentionally left blank.

Listen-Focus-Respect
Make It Real!

The Listen-Focus-Respect matrix is a useful tool. It enables you to create an instructional model to use as you teach the attitudes, skills and habits of Listen-Focus-Respect.

	Show *Model all the time*	**Tell** *Teach with direct instruction*	**Do** *Practice in supportive settings*	**Independence** *Encourage students to do it on their own*	**Connect** *Take the new skills into other settings*
Listen	• Make Time • Active Listening • Eye Contact • Nonverbal and Verbal Encouragement	• Describes the SLANT Steps to Listening • Play Listening Games • Read • Paraphrase	• Play Listening Games • Ask for Active Listening • Offer Active Listening • Connect and Communicate	• Allow him/her to Listen on his/her own • Recognize and Praise Listening • Ask him/her to Teach it to Others	• Associate Listening to school, social, familial, and career success.
Focus	• Eye Contact • Set Classroom Routines • Set Classroom Goals and Priorities • Value Relationships	• Hold Class Meetings • Talk About Priorities and Goals	• Allow Students to Contribute • Adhere to Classwork and Homework Routines	• Allow Students to Develop Interests and Activities	• Associate Focus to school, social, familial, and career success.
Respect	• Respect Yourself • Say What You Mean. Mean What you Say • Set Limits • Use Respectful Language	• Set Limits • Describe Respectful Language • Discuss Respect for Self and Others	• Use Respectful Language Everyday • Maintain Healthy Habits • Adhere to Limits	• Make Student Responsible for Self Care • Allow for appropriate Decision Making Opportunities	• Associate Respect to school, social, familial, and career success.

This page intentionally left blank.

The Research of Beat for Peace

World Music Drumming
Resiliency & Efficacy
National Standards for Music Education
ASCA Student Competencies

This page intentionally left blank.

World Music Drumming Key Concepts	National Standards for Music Education	Characteristics of Resiliency & Efficacy	ASCA Student Competencies
Respect	Singing, alone and with others, a varied repertoire of music.	Social Competence	Academic A: Students will acquire the attitudes, knowledge and skills that contribute to effective learning across the life span
Focus		Empathy & Caring	
Teamwork	Performing on instruments, alone and with others, a varied repertoire of music.	Communication Skills	
Complement		Problem Solving	Academic C: Students will understand the relationship of academics to the world of work, and to life at home and in the community
Listen	Improvising melodies, variations, and accompaniments.	Flexible Thinking	
Call & Response		Reflectivity	
Musical Space	Composing and arranging music within specified guidelines.	Autonomy & Independence	Personal Social A: Students will acquire the knowledge, attitudes, and interpersonal skills to help them understand and respect self and others
Communication		Sense of Identity	
Community	Listening to, analyzing, and describing music.	Internal Locus of Control	
Compliment		Sense of Purpose & Future	
Tone Quality	Evaluating music and music performances.	Optimism	Personal Social C: Students will understand safety and survival Skills
Watch	Understanding relationships between music, the other arts, and disciplines outside the arts.	Goal Directedness	
Balance		Achievement Orientation	Career C: Students will understand the relationship between personal qualities, education, training and the world of work.
	Understanding music in relation to history and culture.		

This page intentionally left blank.

Why Beat for Peace?

Anticipated Student Outcomes

This page intentionally left blank.

Why Beat for Peace?

Students who participate in Beat for Peace **show:**

- **Improved Attendance**

- **Better Grades**

- **Fewer Discipline Incidents**

- **Greater School Commitment**

- **Positive Teacher Report**

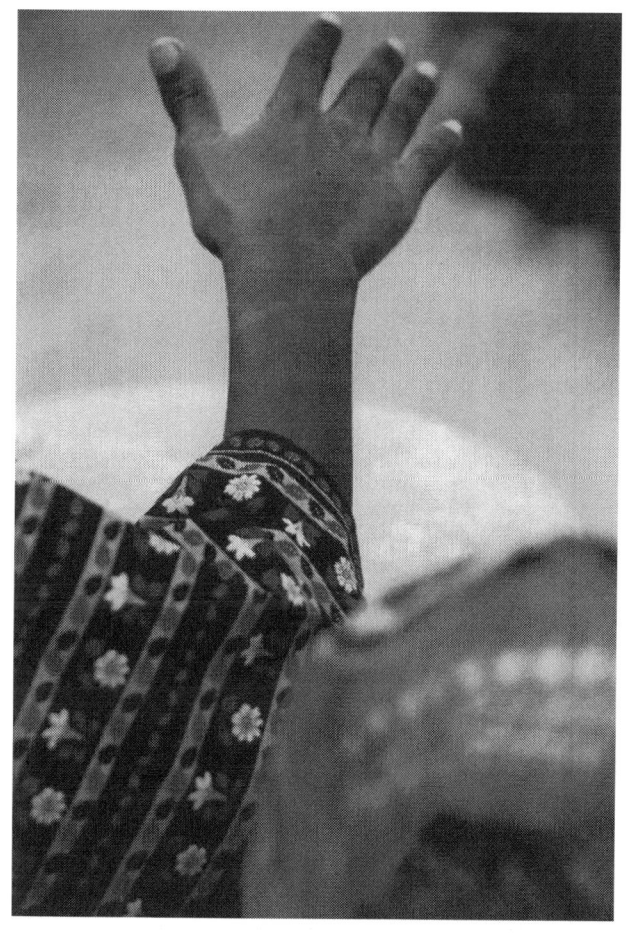

Photo Credit: Ann Newmann

This page intentionally left blank.

DUNNO
The Talking Drum Lessons

This page intentionally left blank.

Lesson: **Section:**

#1 Welcome Session

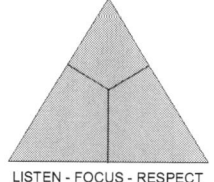

Overview:
Students are welcomed to the drum ensemble. Congratulations are extended. Rehearsal and DUNNO schedules are discussed. Permission slips and related documents are provided.

Links:
MUSIC –

Play and/or discuss drum circle music. Examples include: *Skins, Sticks and Bars* (Paul Corbiere), *Naa-Miami* (Sowah Mensah), *Planet Drum* (Mickey Hart), and/or *Caribbean Playground* (Putumayo Kids).

LISTEN/FOCUS/RESPECT –

Present and discuss your attention signal as the way leaders call out to others in order to get their attention and participation. We use *ago-ame*. The *ago* call roughly translates to "Are you with me?" The *ame* response roughly translates to "Yes, we are with you." The adult leader calls *ago*. The students respond *ame* and then stop talking and freeze. Practice it until the response is in unison and all speaking and movement cease.

RESILIENCY SKILL DEVELOPMENT –

Establish an environment of caring and support. Describe how you and the other adult sponsor(s) are now available to the student drummers. Discuss how the students were chosen from a list of many interested persons.

Materials:
- Drum circle music such as *Skins, Sticks and Bars* (Paul Corbiere), *N aa-Miami* (Sowah Mensah), *Planet Drum* (Mickey Hart), and/or *Caribbean Playground* (Putumayo Kids).
- Permission slips.
- Literature, story book or video of a world music drum ensemble. Accuracy is important.

Procedure:

SAY: Introduce yourself and the other adult sponsor(s) and welcome the student drummers to the drum ensemble.

DO: Practice *ago-ame* or your own attention signal.

DO: Using music and literature, discuss the long tradition of drum circles.

SAY: Review the rehearsal and DUNNO schedules.

DO: Distribute permission slips. Be sure to set a deadline for parent consent.

SAY: *Congratulations on being selected from a sea of candidates. You have been invited to be a part of one of the coolest groups in school! Thank you and I look forward to seeing you next time.*

Related Quote/Literature:

Beat the Story Drum, Pum-Pum (Aladdin Books)
The Leopard's Drum: An Asante Tale from West Africa

Comments:

The first session sets the tone for the rest of the year. Strike a balance between fun and respect. Review and practice the *ago-ame* call and response until you get 100% participation.

Lesson: **Section:**

#2 Hello Bongo

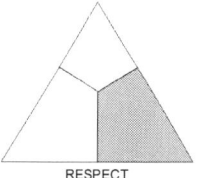
RESPECT

Overview:
Students are welcomed back to the drum ensemble, Today's focus will be on getting to know one another with special emphasis being placed on respect for diversity using the *Hello Bongo* activity page.

Links:
MUSIC –

While in the drum circle, play a question-answer pattern and vary the question to include "what's your name?"; "who's your teacher?" or any other question that can reveal personal information. While in small group counseling, ask these questions again. Use the group process to encourage students to interact, comment and respond to one another.

LISTEN/FOCUS/RESPECT –

Students demonstrate respect for one another in various ways during the *Hello Bongo* activity. Before beginning, discuss the appropriate way to introduce oneself to another. Be sure to appreciate the cultural traditions of your students and be sensitive to shy or withdrawn students. Use the activity to celebrate the items that the group has in common as well as those traits or experiences unique to one or two persons.

RESILIENCY SKILL DEVELOPMENT –

Social competence, communication skills, and the ability to introduce oneself are essential characteristics of the resilient child. *Hello Bongo* provides a non-threatening environment for students to learn, practice and/or model these traits.

Materials:
- *Hello Bongo* Activity Sheet
- *Student Pre-Survey* (Forms and Tools section of this book)
- Clipboards and pencils

Procedure:

SAY: *Welcome back* everybody! Praise the prompt return of permission slips.

DO: Distribute the *Hello Bongo* Activity Sheet, clipboards and pencils. Students must introduce themselves to each other, find someone who meets the description in each of the boxes, and write their names in the corresponding box. Stress the importance of using respectful behavior and manners. Demonstrate or role play how to introduce oneself in social situations.

SAY: *How did you feel introducing yourself? When you found someone else with a common description how did you feel? What do you know now that you did not know before? What do we have in common? How are we unique?*

Related Quote/Literature:

You never get a second chance to make a first impression.
--unknown

Life is partly what we make it and partly what is made by the friends we choose.
--Tennessee Williams

Comments:

Be a participant in *Hello Bongo* too! Walk around, socialize and make connections whenever possible. Be sure to point out how much the group has in common.

Hello Bongo

Step 1: Find someone who fits the description listed below.
Step 2: Face the other person and say "Hello, my name is____, what is your name?"
Step 3: Write their name in the box.

Someone who has been to Walt Disney World.	Someone born the same month as you.	Someone who wears glasses.	Someone who likes mushrooms on their pizza.
Someone who has (or had) the same teacher as you.	Someone who knows how to spell responsibility.	Someone with the same hair color as you.	Someone with the same favorite food as you.
Someone who made an A or B on their last school test.	Someone who was in the Drum Circle last year.	Someone with the same number of family members as you.	Someone who knows the motto of the Drum Circle.

This page intentionally left blank.

Lesson: **Section:**

#3 Drum Compact
Listen-Focus-Respect

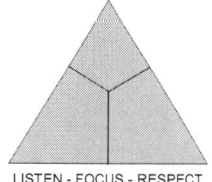
LISTEN - FOCUS - RESPECT

Overview:
People work better when they understand what they are working for. During today's activities, students will see the "big picture" of the drum ensemble. Spending time on the Beat for Peace Instructional Model will make evident the role these skills play in academic life (as a learner and with teachers or authority figures), family life (with parents and/or guardians) and social life (with friends and peers). This lesson guarantees that participants understand that we learn drum ensembles and develop life skills. The **Listen-Focus-Respect** skill set is interdependent and success in one area is dependent on success in the others. Drumming helps us to develop and practice **Listen-Focus-Respect**. Our ability to practice **Listen-Focus-Respect** makes it possible for us to learn drums ensembles. The two complement one another.

Links:

MUSIC –

Select a drum ensemble or piece that demonstrates complementary relationships between instruments. The World Music Drumming: A Cross Cultural Curriculum and Video (Will Schmid) demonstrates this concept throughout its seven ensembles.

LISTEN/FOCUS/RESPECT –

A sound foundation in the ability to practice **Listen-Focus-Respect** will provide both immediate and long term benefit. Review the *ago-ame* call to demonstrate the concept. Brainstorm how **Listen-Focus-Respect** can benefit us today (learning in the classroom, understanding the directions of school principal, keeping friends, etc).

RESILIENCY SKILL DEVELOPMENT –

By spending time on the Beat for Peace Instructional Model, we are pinpointing three areas in the development of the resilient child. Students are introduced to social competence, empathy & caring, and communication skills. Further development in these areas occurs later as more work is done in the individual areas of Communication, Developing Focus through Goal Setting, and Demonstrating Respect.

Materials:
- Slide or Overhead of the Beat for Peace Instructional Model
- *Drum Compact* Activity Sheet
- Clipboards, crayons and pencils
- *World Music Drumming* Video (ensemble 1) or other drum ensemble demonstrating complementary patterns.

Procedure:
SAY: Welcome everyone back.

DO: Display the *Beat for Peace Instructional Model* Slide or Overhead.

SAY: *Beat for Peace is supposed to teach us about drum ensembles, various cultures, and real life skills. Look at the overhead showing the **Listen-Focus-Respect** triangle. The ability to Listen, Stay Focused and to Demonstrate Respect is essential in everyday life and in the process of making music.*

DO: Discuss The 6 Keys and how the core attitudes, skills and habits of **Listen-Focus-Respect** are complementary.

DO: Brainstorm how **Listen-Focus-Respect** can help in learning a drum ensemble. Play *World Music Drumming* ensemble 1 or equivalent and discuss the role that these skills play in learning the piece. Continue to brainstorm to include application in the school setting, at home, and with friends and peers. Be sure that the students include responses like:

<u>Listening</u>
- Helps me to learn my part.
- Helps me learn math (science, reading, etc).
- Keeps me safe (fire drills, home safety).
- Keeps me out of trouble (with my parents, teachers, friends).

<u>Focus</u>
- I have to pay attention to learn.
- I have to pay attention at home so I know what my parents want me to do.
- I have to pay attention to the important things (the social studies lecture) and not pay attention to things like my friend passing me a note.

<u>Respect</u>
- It is important to say "please" and "thank you".
- Respect your elders (parents, teachers, friends).
- If you respect yourself, then others will respect you.

DO: Distribute the *Drum Compact*, clipboards, and pencils. Read and complete the activity as a group.

SAY: *The Drum Compact holds us accountable for our school grades, behavior, and attendance. Your teacher will sign it as well.*

DO: Obtain signatures from the student, homeroom teacher and drum circle sponsor(s). Photocopy and share the compact with the student and his(her) teacher. Retain a copy.

Optional Activity: Based on the life experiences of your student population the following optional activity might be beneficial. You can draw from activities outside of music. In this example, I will use the team sport of soccer.

DO: Brainstorm how **Listen-Focus-Respect** can help in learning soccer. Brainstorm and list what the group knows about soccer (rules, players, positions, etc). Discuss the role that these skills play in learning the game. Continue the brainstorm to include application in the school setting, at home, and with friends and peers. Be sure that the students include responses like:

<u>Listening</u>
- Helps me to learn from the coach.
- Helps me to know what the other players are doing.
- Keeps me safe by hearing the referee's whistle.
- Keeps me out of trouble (with my parents, teachers, friends).

<u>Focus</u>
- I have to pay attention to the game to score goals.
- I have to pay attention to the game or I can get hit by the ball.
- I have to pay attention to the important things (the game) and not pay attention to things like the fans or the other team's players trying to distract me.

<u>Respect</u>
- It is important to be a good sport if we win or lose.
- It is important to respect the game by playing by the rules.
- If you respect yourself, then others will respect you.

Related Quote/Literature:
I learned that respect, focus and teamwork is better then having disrespect, nonfocus, and selfishness.
--Beat for Peace Drummer

Comments:
Listen-Focus-Respect will quickly become the group's motto. You'll say "Listen" and they finish with "Focus-Respect." Get used to using the three words together as if they were one.

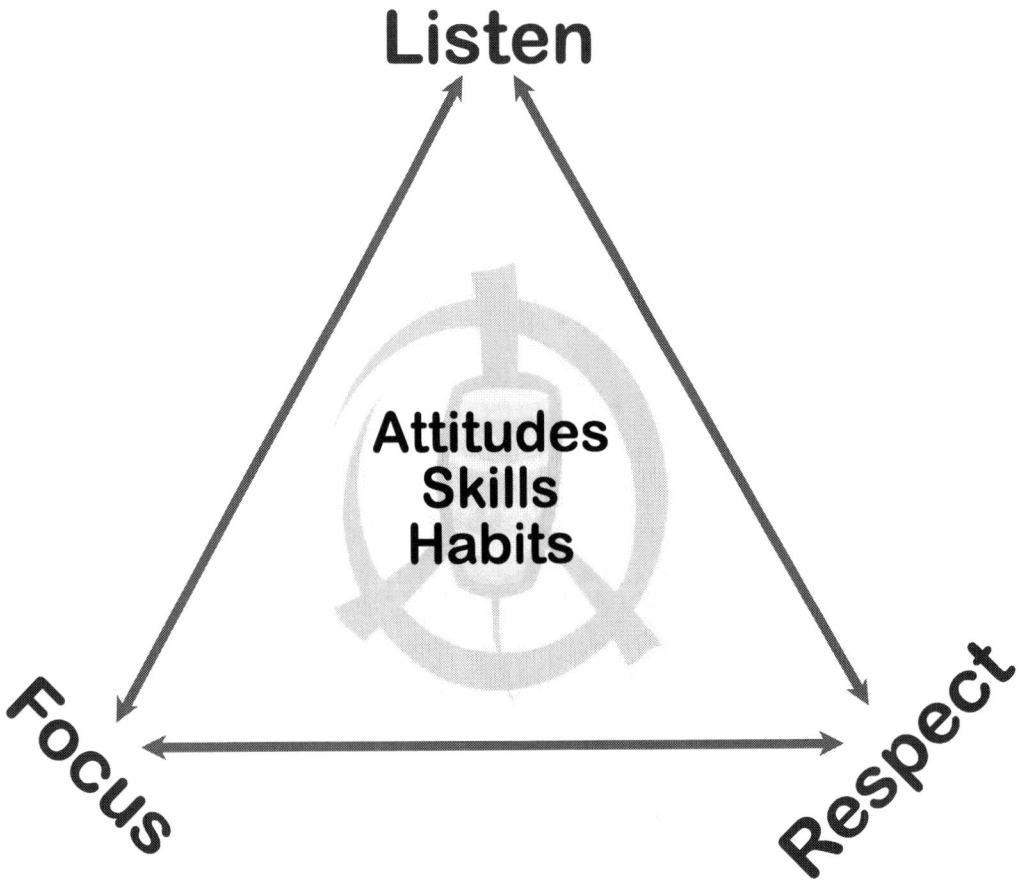

The 6 Keys

1. **LISTEN-FOCUS-RESPECT** are interconnected.

2. **LISTEN-FOCUS-RESPECT** leads to academic success.

3. **LISTEN-FOCUS-RESPECT** leads to successful relationships with families, peers, teachers and authority figures.

4. **LISTEN-FOCUS-RESPECT** leads to college and career readiness.

5. **LISTEN-FOCUS-RESPECT** can be modeled, taught, and encouraged.

6. Students come to us with different attitudes, levels of skill, and a mixture of good and bad habits. We can improve the ability of students to **LISTEN-FOCUS-RESPECT**.

Drum Ensemble Compact

As a proud member of the **Drum Ensemble**, I agree to:

Listen:

- Look at my teacher and any adult when they are speaking.
- Wait for my turn or permission before speaking.
- Follow my teacher's or any adult's direction first time given.
- Ask questions when I do not understand what I have heard.
- Hear the sound and silence the drum ensemble makes when we play.

Focus:

- Look at my teacher and any adult when they are speaking.
- Complete work assignments immediately.
- Understand what is being said.
- Avoid being distracted by things that matter least.
- Understand the meaning behind the drum ensemble.

Respect:

- Look at my teacher and any adult when they are speaking.
- Use manner words when talking with others.
- Use careful actions with others inside and outside the drum ensemble.
- Come to the drum Ensemble with care and ready to play.

_____   _____   _____   _____
Drum Ensemble Member Date   Classroom Teacher   Date

_____   _____   _____   _____
Name/Position   Date   Name/Position   Date

This page intentionally left blank.

Lesson: **Section:**

#4 Decorate Your Drum

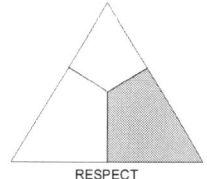
RESPECT

Overview:
This lesson is dedicated to developing a strong sense of self. Previous lessons celebrated respect for others and the value to diversity. During today's activities, students will develop self-awareness using the *Decorate Your Drum* activity page. A key element in the activity is to introduce the concept of maintaining a positive attitude & optimism. The practice of positive self-talk in introduced. Students will be asked to find their own personal theme song – music that brings forth feelings of confidence.

Links:
MUSIC –
Provide various samples of theme songs with optimistic and empowering themes. Examples could include *We Are the Champions* by Queen, *Indiana Jones: Raiders of the Lost Ark* theme, *Leia's Theme (Star Wars)*, *RESPECT* by Aretha Franklin, *Walking on Sunshine* by Katrina and the Waves, or *The Sharing Song* by Jack Johnson. Be prepared with current titles and performers. Don't be afraid to pull from current hits / pop radio.

LISTEN/FOCUS/RESPECT –
Students demonstrate respect for oneself during the *Decorate Your Drum* activity. Before beginning, discuss how to introduce yourself and how to be a good listener while waiting on your turn to share. The focus on positive thinking, positive behavior, as well as the celebration of special skills allows for participants to experience self-respect.

RESILIENCY SKILL DEVELOPMENT –
An internal locus of control, strong sense of self, and belief in purpose and future are essential characteristics of the resilient child. The efficacious student is aware of his or her strengths and areas in need of growth. She believes that she can learn and has a plan to do so.

Materials:
- *Decorate Your Drum* Activity Page
- Clipboards, crayons and pencils
- Various songs or compact discs.

Procedure:

SAY: Welcome everyone back.

DO: Distribute the *Decorate Your Drum* activity page, clipboards, crayons and pencils. Students are to decorate their drum in anyway they choose as long as they answer the following questions:
- What is your name?
- What is your favorite color?
- What activity are you best at?
- Who is your real life hero? Why?
- What kind of music makes you feel confident and strong? Or What do you say to yourself to make yourself feel confident and strong?

SAY: *The drum can be decorated using any colors, words or pictures. Your drum should represent you, just like a family coat of arms represents a family.*

DO: Have students share their drum with the group. In larger groups, you might consider a pair:share interaction.

SAY: *How did you feel introducing yourself? What was it like to say something positive about yourself? Some people are reluctant to speak about themselves for fear that it might be considered boastful. What do you all think?*

DO: Discuss the power of positive thinking. Give a few examples of positive self-talk. Link self-talk to our ability to set and reach goals (hopes and dreams). Self-talk will be explored in more detail later on. At this point keep it short and sweet.

SAY: *Between now and our next session, find some music that can become your own personal theme song. Remember, theme songs are usually are played when the heroine is beating the bad guy. Your theme song should provide you with a boost of inner strength to help you overcome life's challenges as you reach your hopes and dreams.*

Related Quote/Literature:

Be who you are and say what you feel because those who mind don't matter and those who matter don't mind.
-- Dr. Seuss

If you think you can do a thing or think you can't do a thing, you're right.
--Henry Ford

Consider the heritage of your students and look for literature that discusses family, culture and pride in a manner meaningful to you students.

Decorate Your Drum

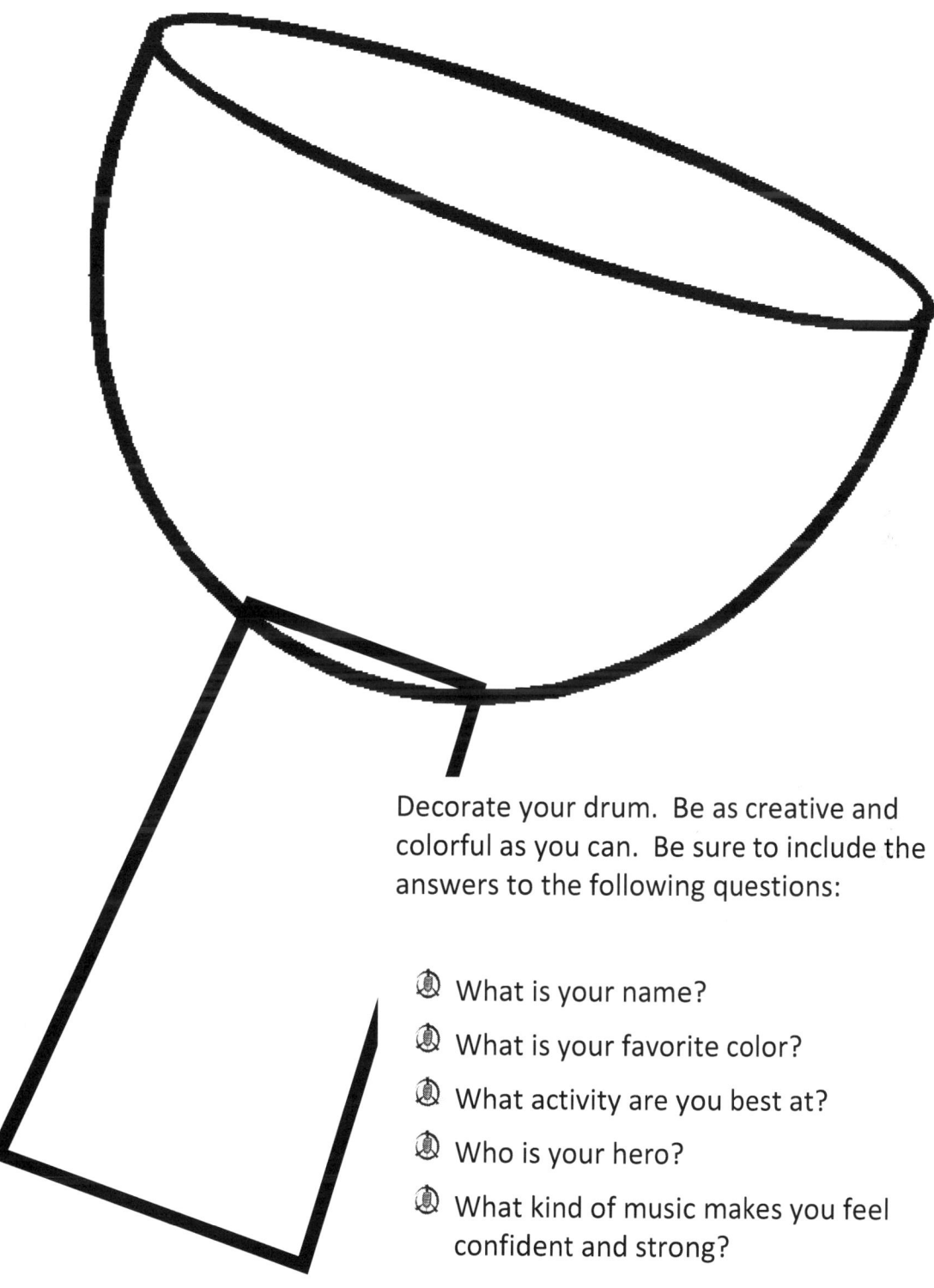

Decorate your drum. Be as creative and colorful as you can. Be sure to include the answers to the following questions:

- What is your name?
- What is your favorite color?
- What activity are you best at?
- Who is your hero?
- What kind of music makes you feel confident and strong?

This page intentionally left blank.

Lesson: **Section:**

#5
Student Pre-Survey

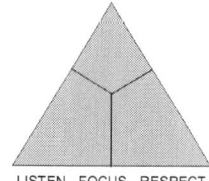
LISTEN - FOCUS - RESPECT

Overview:
The *Student Pre-Survey* should be administered during the first month of the Beat for Peace intervention. The survey will provide baseline data for comparison once the post survey is administered. The Pre-Survey was written to rate the student's perception of him/herself in terms of the characteristics of a resilient child. The survey can also be used to identify data trends that warrant discussion. For example, if a majority of students report that they HARDLY EVER or NEVER stand up for themselves without putting others down (#2), then additional lessons on assertiveness, I-messages and mistreatment/bullying may be appropriate. I recommend the survey items be read to avoid any anxiety about the reading level.

Links:
MUSIC –
Find and play a music CD such as *NTOA* (Sowah Mensah), which is traditional music from Ghana. There is also a wealth of music available on YouTube. Be sure to preview it prior to using.

LISTEN/FOCUS/RESPECT –
Use this opportunity to discuss the value in self-reflection evaluating **Listen-Focus-Respect**. Students should use the survey as an opportunity to reflect on their own attitudes, skills and behaviors; and to make a plan to address disturbing trends. Be sure to celebrate successes.

RESILIENCY SKILL DEVELOPMENT –
The survey questions tap into many of the characteristics of a resilient child such as problem solving, reflectivity, goal directedness, optimism, and an internal locus of control. Spend time discussing items 16, 17, and 18 in relation to personal goals and positive self-talk.

Materials:
- *Student Pre-Survey* Activity Page found in the Forms and Tools section of this manual.
- Clipboards and pencils

Procedure:

SAY: Welcome everyone back.

DO: Distribute the *Student Pre-Survey* activity page, clipboards and pencils.

SAY: *The Student Pre-Survey is completed by you as a way to explore your own successes, areas for improvement, and hopes and dreams for the future. This is a survey and not evaluative. It is not a test and there are no right or wrong answers – only your honest response is required* (I reassure my students that the results are confidential and will not be shared with their teachers.).

DO: Have students complete the surveys. Depending on the reading level, consider reading each item aloud. Collect the surveys and review the data a later time.

SPECIAL NOTE: At times students may disclose information or respond to items in a way that requires follow up. Be sure to meet individually with any students with concerning responses. Work with and involve your school counselor to insure an appropriate response.

DO: Discuss the power of positive thinking as it pertains to the pre-survey questions. Pay particular attention to items 16-18. Give a few examples of positive self-talk. Link self-talk to our ability to set and reach goals (hopes and dreams). Self-talk will be explored in more detail later on. At this point keep it short and sweet.

SAY: *If you have not already found your own personal theme song, keep looking. Remember, theme songs are usually are played when the heroine is beating the bad guy. Your theme song should provide you with a boost of inner strength to help you overcome life's challenges as you reach your hopes and dreams.*

Related Quote/Literature:

Today you are You, that is truer than true. There is no one alive who is Youer than You.
--Dr. Seuss

Comments:

At times students may disclose information or respond to items in a way that requires follow up. Be sure to meet individually with any students who may be in need. Work with and involve your professional school counselor to insure an appropriate response to the student's need.

Lesson:

#6
The Powerful Positive Attitude

Section:

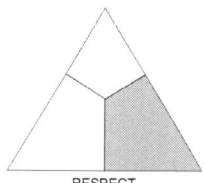

Overview:

Your living is determined not so much by what life brings to you as by the attitude you bring to life; not so much by what happens to you as by the way your mind looks at what happens.
- **John Homer Miller**

The awesome power of positive self-talk and an optimistic attitude is the focus. It is my belief (and the belief of many who explore resiliency and self-efficacy) that the first and most effective step in improving performance is to model, teach and encourage a healthy sense of optimism and belief that one can learn and succeed. Call it confidence. Call it self-esteem. Call it a healthy sense of self. The student is specifically taught to flip negative self-talk statements to the more positive alternative. Students are specifically taught to challenge irrational beliefs and to replace them with healthy rational beliefs.

Links:

MUSIC –

Have your own personal theme song ready to play. Think about the songs that make you want to jump and sing. *Hero* (Chad Kroeger) from the movie *Spiderman* is a great theme song. Discuss how you feel and what you think when you hear your song.

LISTEN/FOCUS/RESPECT –

Use this opportunity to discuss how managing one's own attitude leads to heightened self-respect and better personal relationships. Students should be aware of how their thinking impacts how they feel and perform on specific tasks. *No Stinkin' Thinkin'!*

RESILIENCY SKILL DEVELOPMENT –

A strong sense of optimism and belief in one's ability to succeed are essential characteristics of the resilient child. The efficacious student is aware of his or her strengths and areas in need of growth. When challenged, she/he can maintain a positive attitude through positive self-talk statements.

Materials:
- *Self-Talk*, and *What's Your Attitude?* Pages either copies or projected..
- Any challenging paper & pencil task (ex. a maze copied on both sides of the paper works well)
- Clipboards and pencils
- Your own personal theme song on compact disk or tape.

Procedure:
SAY: Welcome everyone back.

DO: Distribute the maze activity page and direct the students to find their way from start to finish. Once everyone has completed the maze, ask them to turn the paper over and to trace the second maze using their non-dominant hand.
Special Note: Pay careful attention to the student's body language and verbal comments as they complete the task. Many students make negative self-talk statements like "I can't" or "This is too hard" when asked to use their non-dominant hand.

SAY: *Many of you solved the maze easily when you used your dominant hand. I noticed a change when the activity became more difficult when you had to use your non-dominant hand. What did you feel the second time? How was that different from the first time? What were you thinking? What did you say?*

SAY: *Some of you thought that completing the maze with your non-dominant hand was too hard and said to your self "I can't do it". You may have felt frustrated. You had a difficult time doing the maze. This in turn, reinforced the negative self talk. The cycle continues like the spinning wheels of a bicycle.*

DO: Discuss the impact of holding a negative attitude (thoughts, words, actions, feelings). Discuss how thinking impacts feelings, which in turn impacts our performance on tasks. Refer back to the maze example. Display *What's Your Attitude* Activity Sheet. Think of other examples of when negative self-talk can sabotage efforts to complete a task. I use examples like, a child's trip to the zoo:
- Thinking – *The zoo is stupid.*
- Feeling – *bored, frustrated, grumpy, close-minded*
- Doing – *acts grumpy, gets into trouble for "bad attitude", reinforces the idea that the zoo is stupid*

SAY: *It is very important to maintain a positive attitude even in difficult situations. We must persevere, be patient and use self-control.*

DO: Display the *Who's in Charge?* Activity Sheet. Cover the positive self-talk statements, showing on the negative self-talk statements. Discuss each negative statement and when someone might say that. Have the student restate or flip it into a positive statement. Reveal the positive statements as you go. Discuss how a positive self-talk statement can lead to a better result.

SAY: *When might someone say "I'm a big dummy"* (when they make a mistake or get a bad grade). *How could we flip that negative attitude into a positive attitude?* (*I am Smart!*)

DO: Display and discuss the *What's Your Attitude?* transparency page. Emphasize the fact that individuals can control, guide and manage their own attitudes through self-talk statements.

DO: Play your own personal theme song and share how it affects your thoughts, feelings, and behavior.

Related Quote/Literature:

Be very careful about what you think. Your thoughts run your life.
--King Solomon

Anybody Can Bake a Cake by Hennie Shore, Beth Ann Marcozzi, and Lawrence Shapiro

Don't Feed the Monster on Tuesdays by Adolph Moser

Comments:

I find that this lesson works best with plenty of discussion and role play. Students love to brainstorm television characters that use positive self-talk (optimist) and negative self-talk (pessimist). We often talk about developing a positive attitude over several small group sessions. I encourage you to adjust the flow and pacing to meet the needs of your student population.

What's Your Attitude?
Negative Example

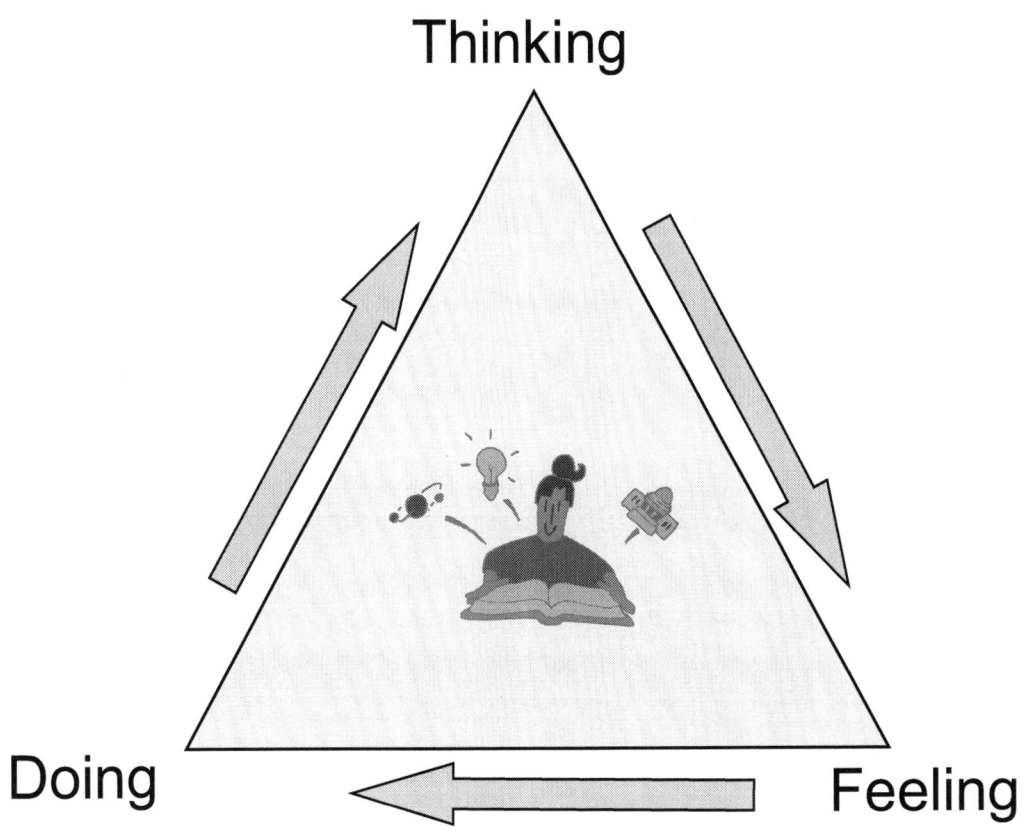

What You Think...   I'm no good at math...

Effects How You Feel...   I feel anxious...

Effects What You Do...   Give up on math test...

Effects What You Think   I knew that I was no good at math!

and so on, and so on...   I feel anxious & stupid...

What's Your Attitude?
Positive Example

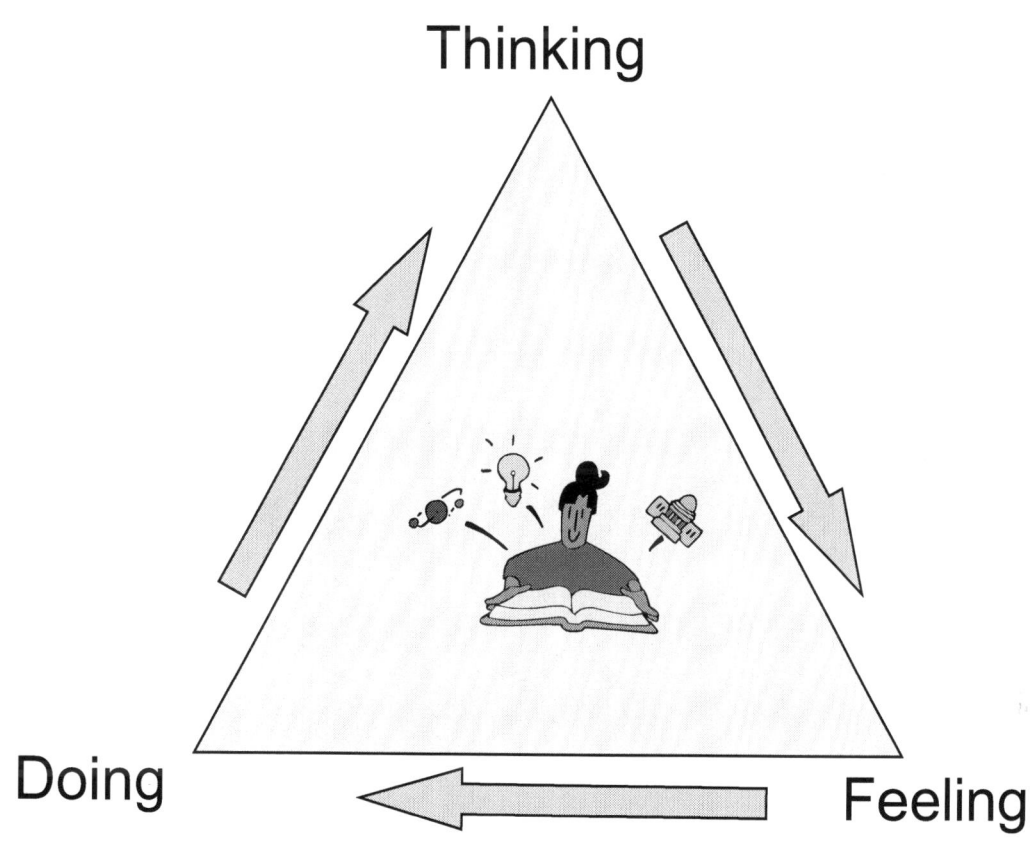

What You Think...	*I will do my best...*
Effects How You Feel...	*I feel confident...*
Effects What You Do...	*Try hard on math test...*
Effects What You Think	*I knew I could do it!*
and so on, and so on...	*I feel proud & happy*

Who's in Charge?
Managing Your Self-Talk

Negative Self-Talk (Pessimism)	Positive Opposite (Optimism)
I'm a big dummy!	*I am smart!*
I don't care!	*I care about this,*
This is stupid!	*This is interesting!*
Easy come easy go!	*This is important.*
I can't do anything right.	*It's OK to make mistakes.*

Think of self-talk as your own personal theme song that plays in your head. Depending on the theme song you "play", you can feel

- confident, strong, and happy
- sad, weak, and depressed
- angry, short tempered, and miserable.

When you find yourself listening to negative self-talk, flip it! Tell yourself the positive opposite. You try it!

Negative Self-Talk	Positive Opposite
This test is too hard! People will make fun of me.	

Lesson:

#7
Hopes and Dreams

Section:

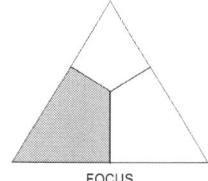
FOCUS

Overview:
Kids love to have Hopes and Dreams. From a resiliency standpoint, students do a better job overcoming risk when they have a sense of purpose and optimism towards the future. Most students have fun talking about their dreams. For that matter, most adults have fun too. This is a great lesson to let your guard down and talk about what you dream about doing. The sky is the limit so share your dreams of being an astronaut (my personal favorite), or visiting the Great Wall of China, or becoming a veterinarian. Dream it, visualize it and plan for it!

Links:
MUSIC –

A very moving compact disc is <u>Facing Forward</u> by Israel Kamakawiwo'ole. The songs tell a story of IZ's dreams for his Hawaiian homeland.

LISTEN/FOCUS/RESPECT –

Use this opportunity to remind everyone of the importance of a positive attitude. Being positive, focused and patient are keys to reaching our dreams. A key element is to drive home the idea that NO ONE can take away our Hopes and Dreams unless we give them permission.

RESILIENCY SKILL DEVELOPMENT –

Developing a Sense of Purpose and Future as well as being Optimistic about one's chances of reaching his/her dreams is our focus in this lesson. Once we can get a student to visualize a future *and* then be optimistic about the same, we're home free. Combining these characteristics with goal setting practice creates a very powerful force for positive self-growth and achievement.

Materials:

- *Hopes and Dreams* activity sheet.
- Examples of successful persons who reached their Hopes and Dreams. Examples could include Henry Ford, Thomas Edison, Michael Jordan, Colin Powell, or even those parents and family members closer to home.
- Clipboards and pencils

Procedure:

Before the Session: This session can be very powerful if you use current examples of people who have been successful in reaching their *Hopes and Dreams*. Be prepared to help your students brainstorm and list their Hopes and Dreams. Be ready to encourage them to expand their dreams beyond "professional football player", "win the lottery" or "famous singer".

SAY: *Everyone has Hopes and Dreams. Hopes and Dreams are those things you would like to learn, do, or achieve. Imagine that the sky is the limit. What are your Hopes and Dreams?* Brainstorm and list examples. Be prepared to offer your own *Hopes and Dreams* to aid the discussion.

DO: Explain to the students that it is important to picture themselves reaching their Hopes and Dreams. Help them to really see it in their mind's eye. *What would it look like to live that dream?* Having a positive and optimistic outlook is essential.

DO: Distribute the *Hopes and Dreams* Activity Sheet. Have the students complete the front of the activity sheet. Be sure that they list their Hopes and Dreams and draw a picture of what it would look like once they reach their dreams.

SAY: *What kinds of things can keep you from reaching your Hopes and Dreams?* Brainstorm potential distracters such as not paying attention in school, using drugs or alcohol, negative peer pressure, getting into trouble, or having a negative (pessimistic) attitude. *Making bad or destructive decisions can keep you from reaching your Hopes and Dreams. What will you do to avoid these pitfalls?* Brainstorm strategies such as paying attention in school, eating healthy foods, being positive and optimistic, get help when you need it, or be responsible. Be sure to connect current choices to future successes.

DO: Complete the back of the activity sheet. Be sure that every student identifies at least one distracter and lists at least one strategy to avoid the pitfall.

Related Quote/Literature:

I've missed more than 9000 shots in my career. I've lost almost 300 games. 26 times, I've been trusted to take the game winning shot and missed. I've failed over and over and over again in my life. And that is why I succeed.
--Michael Jordan

While we may not be able to control all that happens to us, we can control what happens inside us.
 --Benjamin Franklin

An optimist is someone who goes after Moby Dick in a rowboat and takes the tartar sauce with him.
 --Zig Ziglar

Salt in His Shoes: Michael Jordan in Pursuit of a Dream by Deloris Jordan & Roslyn M. Jordan

Comments:

The benefit of collaborating with colleagues and community business partners is the ability to expand this lesson into a series of discussions on career development. Utilize local chambers of commerce, the Workforce Alliance, and your professional school counselor to really dig into this topic. Bring in guest speakers, old drummers who are successful in high school, college students, and others.

This page intentionally left blank.

Hopes and Dreams

Everyone has Hopes and Dreams. Use the space below to write about your Hopes and Dreams.

Draw a picture of what it will look like once you reach your Hopes and Dreams.

Hopes and Dreams

Distracters are those destructive decisions that can prevent you from reaching your Hopes and Dreams. List some possible Distracters.

_____

_____

_____

For every Distracter there is a strategy to hold onto your Hopes and Dreams. List what you can do to remain true to your Hopes and Dreams.

_____

_____

_____

Lesson:

#8 Goal Setting

Section:

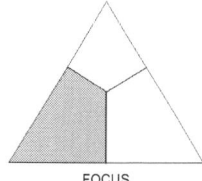
FOCUS

Overview:
Goal setting is one of the more important skills that we address in the intervention. It's where we convert Hopes and Dreams into reality. By teaching the importance of goal setting and the value in celebrating incremental gains, we are able to help students take steps towards greater personal-social and academic success. From a programmatic standpoint, goal setting creates the change that we need as reflected in improved behavior, fewer disciplinary incidents, improved grades, and improved teacher ratings. Return to the key points of the goal setting lessons as frequently as needed to hold students accountable to implementing their goal plans.

Links:

MUSIC –

Reflect back on and/or play the challenging rhythms, parts and ensembles that the group has learned. For example, I had a really tough time learning the timeline part for a particular song. By itself it was simple – just three notes. The challenge was playing the timeline (the three notes) in the right place in the ensemble. That was my goal. I took specific steps (listening to the song on CD, practicing with someone who already mastered the timeline, being focused while learning the ensemble) and persevered in this task. After two years, I have finally figured it out and have enough confidence to teach others.

LISTEN/FOCUS/RESPECT –

Use this opportunity to remind everyone of the importance of a positive attitude. Being positive, focused and patient are keys to goal success.

RESILIENCY SKILL DEVELOPMENT –

I am really drawn to the resiliency skills that address goal directedness and a sense of purpose and future. I find that many of the students I work with have limited view of the future. Very few can talk about their hopes, dreams, and life-education-career pathways. For that matter, many had a tough time identifying short term goals. I believe if I can help students identify short term goals and experience success reaching those goals, then they will be better able to see their own future potential.

Materials:
- *Keep the Beat* goal setting sheet.
- A current calendar or planner for each student.
- Clipboards and pencils

Procedure:

Before the Session: This session can be very powerful if you use real data to help your students make meaningful goal statements. I suggest that you compile current report card grades, standardized assessment data, completed *Teacher Surveys* and the *Drummer Self-Evaluation Form* (Forms and Tools section). Be prepared to help your students identify trends in grades and/or behaviors that might need to be addressed. These can then be identified as individual goal statements.

SAY: *Where would you like to go on a trip?* Brainstorm a list of destinations. Pick one of the destinations to which no one has gone. *What steps will you take to get to this special destination?* Use a map. Ask for directions. Get gasoline. *What would happen if you didn't take these steps?* Get lost. Run out of gas. *What would happen if you never picked a destination? If you never decided where to go, you just went?* You wouldn't know where to go. You would just waste you time.

DO: Explain to the students that goals take us places. Just like planning a big trip, we must first decide where we want to go and then map out the steps to our final destination. Define a goal as something that we want to learn, change, do, or get better at. Goal setting is the process by which we get to where we want to go. Share a goal that you have reached in you own life. Ask students for goals they have reached in their own lives.

SAY: *When you decide what you want to learn, change, do, or get better at, write your goal down. Picture yourself reaching that goal. Take the first step. Everyday we either take steps towards our goal or away from our goal. Reaching our goals requires patience, focus, and persistence.*

DO: Display the activity sheets taking time to discuss each slide. Be sure to address the difference between good specific goal statements and ineffective vague goal statements using the samples included in the transparencies.

SAY: *Now that you know about goal setting think about your own performance. Reflect on your classroom grades, teacher survey comments and own thoughts. Decide what school grade, behavior or relationship that you want to improve upon. Write your goal and the goal steps on your Keep the Beat handout.*

DO: Distribute the *Keep the Beat* goal setting sheet. Be prepared to circulate and assist students in making goal statements based on their data. Verify that the goal statements are specific, measurable, realistic for the student, and timely.

DO: Distribute calendars or refer the students to their daily planners. Discuss the value to recording their progress towards their goal on a daily basis.

Related Quote/Literature:

I do the very best I know how – the very best I can; and I mean to keep doing so until the end…I walk slowly but I never walk backwards.
-- Abraham Lincoln

<u>Salt in His Shoes: Michael Jordan in Pursuit of a Dream</u> by Deloris Jordan & Roslyn M. Jordan

<u>Anybody Can Bake a Cake</u> by Hennie Shore, Beth Ann Marcozzi, and Lawrence Shapiro

Comments:

A common mistake in goal setting is waiting to long before evaluating progress. I've found that most students have a hard time with goal statements like "I want to earn straight A's on my next report card". There are 12 weeks in our trimesters and that's simply too long of a time frame. We get better results when we set goals that include a mechanism for regular (daily or weekly) progress checks. The central question is *Did I work towards my goal <u>today</u> or away from my goal <u>today</u>?*

I often spread this lesson out over two sessions, the first to review the data and the second to generate goal statements. Every DUNNO session from here on out includes a brief goal reporting section for increased accountability.

Hopes and Dreams

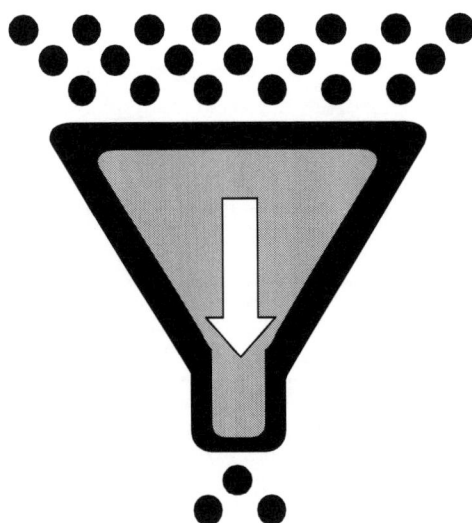

Right Now Goals

Think about your **Hopes and Dreams** from page 71. Think about what you can do <u>right now</u> to take steps toward your dream. Use the space below to write about your Right Now Goal.

Goal Setting

Some Goals...

◈ can be achieved in hours.

◈ take weeks, months, or even years to be achieved!

Your goals should be...

- something you want to learn, change or do.

- Positive.

- Measurable.

- Possible.

Goal Setting Steps

- Decide what you want to learn, change or do.

- Write your goal down.

- Picture yourself reaching the goal.

- List 3 steps you will take to reach your goal.

- Be patient.

Sample Goals

- I will raise my hand in class at least 5 times everyday.

- I will come to school on time (by 8:00AM).

- I will finish my class work on time (or for homework).

- When frustrated, I will not give up!

- I will pay attention in class.

Goal Steps

- Mark down every time I raise my hand.

- Get up at 6:30AM. Set out my clothes the night before.

- I will not talk or daydream in class. Ask to take unfinished work home.

- I will STOP-BREATH-COUNT TO 3.

- I will look at the teacher and pay attention in math.

Month of:_____

Did I Work Towards My Goal Today?

YES

NO

Sunday	Monday	Tuesday	Wednesday	Thursday	Friday	Saturday
☐	☐	☐	☐	☐	☐	☐
☐	☐	☐	☐	☐	☐	☐
☐	☐	☐	☐	☐	☐	☐
☐	☐	☐	☐	☐	☐	☐
☐	☐	☐	☐	☐	☐	☐

My Goal:_____

Keep the Beat
Steps to Making and Keeping Goals

Name: _____

Date: _____

My Goal: _____

_____

Steps I Will Take to Reach My Goal:

1. _____

_____

2. _____

_____

3. _____

_____

I Will Reward Myself for Reaching the Goal by:

_____

_____

_____

This page intentionally left blank.

Lesson:

#9 Communication Skills

Section:

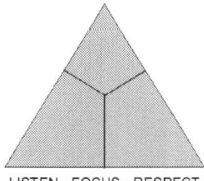
LISTEN - FOCUS - RESPECT

Overview:
The way we communicate with others and with ourselves ultimately determines the quality of our lives.
--Anthony Robbins

Communication skills can be broken down into four (4) interconnected segments: listen to understand, speak clearly, nonverbal messages, and empathy.

Links:

MUSIC –

A very direct connection lies between good listening skills and playing in the drum ensemble. When the drum ensemble leader introduces a new echo pattern, such as *diga diga dat dat*, students must pay attention, actively listen, and have an understanding of the pattern in order to repeat the pattern with accurate rhythm, hand placement and tone.

LISTEN/FOCUS/RESPECT –

Communication hinges on **Listen-Focus-Respect**. In fact, communication is a part of the drum ensemble from day 1. We discuss how listening is essential to the drum circle, important in class and a priority at home. We pose the question "What is the best way to show *respect* for someone?" The answer is, of course, *listen to them*! Finally, just as it is important to play with clarity and meaning, communication includes the ability to speak clearly and with detail.

RESILIENCY SKILL DEVELOPMENT –

Bullying, disenfranchised students, unmotivated learners and the proficiency gap are significant issues in education. By spending time teaching the concepts of empathy and skills of communication we are building positive and ethical relationships with students.

Materials:
- *Communication Diagram* Activity Sheet
- *Roadblocks to Good Communication* Activity Sheet
- *SLANT* Activity Sheet
- *Communication* Activity Sheet
- *Three Tips for Good Communication* Activity Sheet
- *Good Communicator* Game Pieces (1 set, cut out for each person)
- *Non Verbal Communication* Activity Sheet
- *Non Verbal Communication* Cards

Procedure:
When planning this session be prepared for enthusiastic dialogue with students. I often split this topic over several days. I have separated the procedure section into four parts:

Part A: Listen to Understand
Part B: Speak Clearly
Part C: Non Verbal Messages
Part D: Empathy

Related Quote/Literature:

When you talk, you repeat what you already know; when you listen, you often learn something.
-- Jared Sparks

Say what you mean. Mean what you say.
-- unknown

Talk peaceful to be peaceful.
-- Norman Vincent Peal

The True Story of the Three Little Pigs by Jon Scieszka
The Feelings Book by Todd Parr

Comments:
A little prep time pays off with these lessons. Students love to role play and if you gather some short scripts or improvisational scenarios your efforts will be rewarded!

Procedure – Part A: Listen to Understand

Before Part A: Prepare handouts or slides of the *Communication Diagram*, *SLANT*, and *Roadblocks* to communication pages. Have a ready list of conversation topics to supplement the *Communication* Activity Sheet. If possible, locate a video clip or story that demonstrates poor listening. Examples may include a clip of Linus' teacher, Ms. Othmar, from the *Peanuts* series or dialogue between Shrek and Donkey from the *Shrek the Movie*.

SAY: *Anthony Robbins, a successful entrepreneur and strategist, said "The way we communicate with others and ourselves ultimately determines the quality of our lives." What do you think he meant? What do you think communication means?*

The American Heritage Dictionary defines communications
1. The act of communicating; transmission.
2. The exchange of thoughts, messages, or information, as by speech, signals, writing, or behavior. Interpersonal rapport.

*Communication involves **sending the message**, **receiving the message**, and **understanding the message**.*

DO: Display the *Communication Diagram*. Discuss the interdependence between each circle in the diagram.

SAY: *Who has had a time when communication did not work. When you had a misunderstanding? What happened? What do you think went wrong?* Be prepared to share about a time that you did not listen. Brainstorm list of roadblocks to good communication. Be sure to include things that interfere with careful listening. Display *Roadblocks* to Good Communication Overhead.

DO: List common roadblocks to careful listening: not looking at the speaker, moving around, thinking about something other than what is being said, not asking questions, and/or talking while someone else is talking.

DO: Display the *SLANT* Style page discussing how each relates to careful listening.

DO: Place students in teams of two. Distribute the *Communication* activity sheet. One person is the "Sender" and the other is the "Receiver". The Sender will speak clearly on the first topic for one minute. The "Receiver" will listen using SLANT. Process the activity by asking the Senders to rate how well their Receivers listened. Be sure to discuss how it feels to be listened to. Trade positions and repeat using the second topic.

SAY: *The first key to successful relationships is to LISTEN. When we LISTEN with care, we avoid confusion and conflict. When we check ourselves for understanding we learn. Everyone likes to be listened to.*

Procedure – Part B: Speak Clearly

Before Part B: Prepare the Good Communicator game pieces by cutting all of the shapes out. Each student should have a set of the pieces (star, rectangle, triangle, circle, arrow). For an added twist you could copy the pieces using color paper so that they can be identified by shape or color.

SAY: *As we saw last time, listening is only a part of communication. We must also speak clearly and ask questions to understand. Today's game requires us to do just that, speak clearly and ask questions.*

DO: Display the *Roadblocks* to communication handout or slide. Brainstorm ways to avoid roadblocks when sending (speaking) messages. Be sure to include:
1. Speak Clearly,
2. Monitor Tone of Voice, and
3. Give Lots of Details.

DO: Divide the students into pairs. Each pair will have two sets of game pieces. One student will be the speaker/designer and the other student will be the listener/replicator. The students sit back to back with each one having his/her set of game pieces. The speaker creates a design out of the shapes. The speaker should verbally describe the design as he or she makes it. For example, if they place the **star** to the right of the **circle** he/she would say "Place the star to the right of the circle." The listener must listen and ask questions as he/she replicates the design. The students can not look at each other's design during the game. They must rely of listening and speaking skills.

Use the *Three Tips for Good Communication* overhead to encourage the students to speak clearly, listen, focus, and ask questions.

DO: Begin the game and monitor as the student pairs use verbal communication skills to complete the task until everyone is done. Call time and allow the pairs to compare designs.

SAY: *Was this task easy or hard for you? Why? Which pairs came the closest to an exact match? How? Was the speaker sending a clear message? Did the listener stay focused and ask questions?*

DO: Continue to process the game being sure to emphasize how good communication is required for the game. Reverse the roles and repeat the game.

Procedure – Part C: Non Verbal Messages

If you have ever driven on a busy interstate highway during rush hour you have seen how messages can be sent using nonverbal means. In fact, much of what we "say" in communication comes from facial expressions, gestures, body posture, and eye contact. Often, the unspoken part of our communication message carries more weight than the spoken part. How many times have you heard someone say something but their body language delivered an entirely different message?

A great way to start this portion of the lesson is to rely entirely on nonverbal cues to organize the class. For example, you might put your forefinger to your lips to indicate "quiet" or position your hand palm down as you move it down to indicate "sit down."

SAY: *We have already learned about the spoken part of communication and how to use our eyes and ears to listen and understand. Non verbal expressions and movements are a major part of communication. Non verbal communication includes facial expressions, body posture, hand gestures and eye contact.*

SAY: *How many of you have ever rolled your eyes in response to something your parents said?* Acknowledge those who raised their hands. *What happened?* You will get responses like "parents got mad," or "I got in trouble." *What did you "say" to your parents when you rolled your eyes?* Elicit answers like "I don't respect you" or "who cares what you say."

SAY: *That's right you can say a lot with your actions. What am I saying to you now?*
    Index finger to mouth – "Quiet"
    Index finger pointed to head – "Think"
    Arms crossed – "Leave me alone"
    Thumbs up – "Good job"
    Sucking teeth – "Who cares" or "That's stupid"

DO: Introduce the *Non Verbal Communication Card* Game. The game is a lot like charades in which the person who is "it" must use nonverbal means to communicate a feeling or statement. The observer who guesses correctly acts out a message next. You can generate your own statements and feelings or use the attached suggestions.

SAY: *When we monitor our own non verbal cues we can better send a clear message during communication. We can align our words with our actions to create a genuine presence. Being able to read the non verbal cues of others creates better relationships. We can sense when a friend is sad. We can tell if a parent is stressed out and should be left alone. We can read social situations that could turn into hazardous events.*

Procedure – Part D: Empathy

The ability to communicate well with others is enhanced when you share in another's perception. That is when you place yourself in their shoes. The children's book The True Story of the Three Little Pigs is a great story for illustrating this concept. The book takes the reader through the story from the wolf's perspective.

SAY: *Henry Ford, the father of Ford Motorcars said "If there is any one secret to success, it lies in the ability to get the other person's point of view and see things from his angle as well as yours."*

SAY: *Empathy involves viewing the world or a situation from another person's perspective, and being able to understand their feelings in that perspective. You can disagree with that person's perspective and still have empathy.*

DO: Present The True Story of the Three Little Pigs. Take time to discuss the differences in perception. You can illustrate this concept further by displaying common optical illusions that function based on perceptual difference. Popular ones include the Vase or Face illusion or the Young Girl – Old Woman illusion.

DO: Present The Feelings Book. Include discussions of the various feelings being sure to identify times that the students felt that way.

OPTIONAL ACTIVITIES:

There are many ways to explore empathy and feelings. **Feelings Beach Ball** is a game I created by writing various feeling word on a beach ball. Players take turn passing the ball. When the ball is caught the player identifies the feeling word that their hand has touched. He/she must tell of a time they felt that feeling. **Feelings Charades** is just like the Non Verbal Communication game, but limited to feelings.

THE 3 INGREDIENTS FOR EFFECTIVE COMMUNICATION

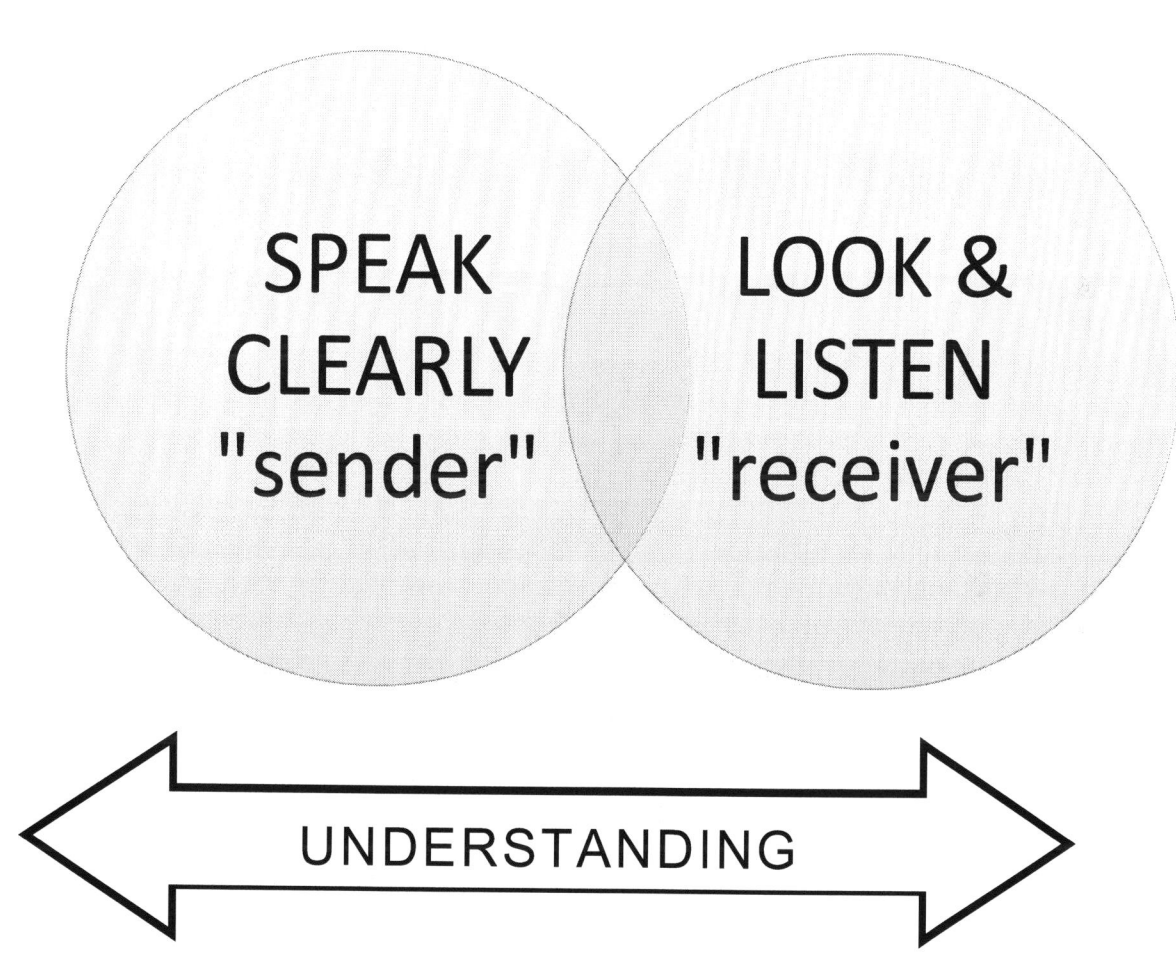

ROADBLOCKS

	Mumbling Fuzzy Messages Tone of Voice Not Giving Details
Not Asking Questions Hearing, NOT Listening Strong Emotions Being Distracted	

Roadblocks disrupt the sending and receiving of important messages and often results in conflict.

SLANT

- Sit Still

- Look at the speaker

- Ask questions

- Nod your head

- Think about what is being said

Communication

Name:_____

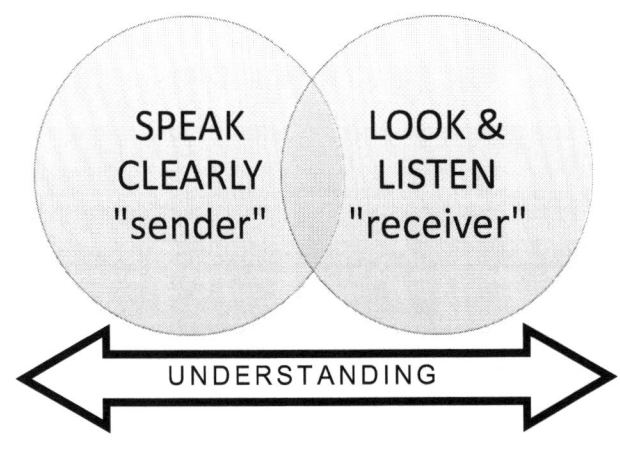

3 TIPS:
Listen

Focus

Ask Questions

What famous person would you like to eat lunch with?
Why would you want to eat with that person?
What would you eat?
What questions would you like to ask that person?

What if you were the first person to land on the new planet Tubanican?
 What would you do? Who would you take with you? Why? What would make the planet a great place to live?

Three Tips for Good Communication

1. Listen

2. Focus

3. Ask Questions

Good Communicator Game Pieces

Non Verbal Communication

- How you say something matters as much as what you say.

- You can say a lot without speaking.

- Body language is important.

- Facial expressions give hints as to how you really think or feel.

How would you use nonverbal Communication to "say" the following?

Hello.
I am frustrated.
Come here.
I don't care what you say!
Disgusting!

Goodbye
I'm bored.
I Won!
I feel scared.
I feel happy.

Non Verbal Communication Cards

I am happy	I am sad
I am angry	I am embarrassed
Come here	Stop
I won!	What's up?
I'm confused	Who cares?
I'm OK	He quiet
Leave me alone	I am lonely
I'm frightened	I am disgusted

Lesson:

#10 Relationships – Friendship Skills

Section:

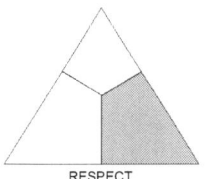
RESPECT

Overview:
Older elementary school students are taking their first steps on the path to adolescence and eventual adulthood. The power of peer relationships in growing day by day. The purpose of this lesson is to spend time discussing healthy friendships, prosocial attitudes, prosocial skills and prosocial behaviors.

Links:
MUSIC –
Remind the students of the complementary rhythms present in ensemble #1 from <u>World Music Drumming</u> and/or *Rock It!* from <u>World Music Drumming: New Ensembles and Songs</u>. Complementary rhythms go together like peanut butter and jelly or Batman and Robin or SpongeBob Squarepants and Patrick.. Brainstorm other common partnerships and discuss how they complement each other.

LISTEN/FOCUS/RESPECT –
Building healthy friendships requires from having respect for yourself and others.

RESILIENCY SKILL DEVELOPMENT –
Resilient people feel connected. Having healthy friendships with peers creates a web of support for when times get tough. Pre-adolescents and teenagers often rely of same age peers more so than adults for social approval, advice support. It is important that connections are positive and healthy.

Materials:
- *What is Friendship?* Activity Sheet
- Dry Erase Board

Procedure:

Before the session: There is a great deal of youth oriented literature on friendships, peer pressure and cliques. I suggest that you pull some books for sharing with your students.

SAY: *What is a good friend?* Ask the students to define a good friend. *Is there such a thing as a bad friend?* Ask the students to define a bad friend.

DO: Create a T-Chart on the board. Distribute the *What is Friendship?* Activity Sheet. Direct the students to fold the paper in ½ (long way like a hot dog bun) and then list the characteristics that they look for in a good friend on their T-Chart. The list will likely include attitudes, skills and behaviors such as funny, athletic, keeps secrets, smart, popular, and nice. On the "Things that make me a good friend" side of the T-Chart, direct the students to list their own characteristics that make them a good friend to others. List their responses on the board. Compare the two sides of the T-chart.

SAY: *Compare the two sides of your T-Chart. What do you notice? Are you a good friend to others?* Discuss similarities to differences between to the two sides of the T-Chart. Discuss the Ralph Waldo Emerson's quote "The only way to have a friend is to be one."

DO: Introduce the concept of bad or unhealthy friendships using literature like Trevor Romain's book Cliques, Phones and Other Baloney. Define cliques as groups that exclude others for silly reasons. Define friendships of convenience as when relationships are based on material possessions (*He's got that new game system, lets go hang with him!*). Discuss unhealthy friendships as those relationships that can lead to very negative consequences such as gang involvement. For more information on gang prevention, check out the United States Department of Justice or your state level Department of Law Enforcement for initiatives and education.

SAY: *Engaging in unhealthy friendships of any kind will have life long consequences. You are who you hang out with.*

Related Quote/Literature:

"What you do is what you get."
--unknown

Chicken Soup for the Teenage Soul on Love and Friendship by Jack Canfield, Mark Hansen, and Kirberger.

Cliques, Phonies and Other Baloney by Trevor Romain.

Comments:
Avoid sounding judgmental of student friendships. Some students may be in unhealthy relationships and may be fearful of being judged by another adult. Others may share stories just to test your reaction. Either way, your response to or follow up on student disclosures will impact the relationship you share.

What is Friendship?

| Things I look for in a good friend | Things that make ME a good friend. |
|---|---|//
| | |

FOLD HERE

What do you notice when you compare both sides of the chart?

_____

_____

Lesson:

#11 Solving Peer Pressure Problems

Section:

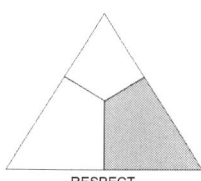
RESPECT

Overview:

On July 11, 1805 Alexander Hamilton and Aaron Burr met on the dueling grounds of Weehawken, New Jersey. By the end of the day Mr. Hamilton was mortally wounded and Aaron Burr escaped without a scratch. How did one of our Founding Fathers, a participant in the Revolutionary War, and George Washington's Treasury Secretary find himself find himself committed to a duel? Peer pressure. By the 1800's dueling was declared illegal in most areas and Mr. Hamilton was known to be opposed to the practice. Nevertheless, when presented with the challenge he responded "what men of the world denominate honor, imposed on me (as I thought) a peculiar necessity not to decline the call." He chose to duel, in part, because it was what some of those around him pressured him to do.

Peer pressure is not new. When used for ethical outcomes, it can be a very honorable and just force. When used in the absence of ethics or with the intent to create harm it can be devastating.

Links:

MUSIC –

Refer back to Lesson #6 The Powerful Positive Attitude and remind the students of their own personal theme song. Having a positive attitude and a clear idea of self empowers the individual to resist Negative Peer Pressure.

LISTEN/FOCUS/RESPECT –

Respect for self is evidenced by making life long healthy choices. Avoiding common destructive emotional and physiological choices that are the product of Negative Peer Pressure demonstrates respect for self. One can argue that smoking, early onset of drug and alcohol use, unprotected sexual intercourse, and/or illegal activity is often initiated in the pressure cooker of negative peer influence.

RESILIENCY SKILL DEVELOPMENT –

A resilient person is known to be autonomous, independent, and guided by intrinsic forces. Having a strong sense of self and the courage to act on that sense can guide us through the decision making process for a positive outcome.

Materials:
- *Stop-Think-Choose* Activity Sheet
- *What to Do* Activity Sheet
- *You Decide…* Activity Sheet

Procedure:
Before the session: Spend some time gathering local information related to peer pressure. With a little searching you should be able to find examples of positive peer pressure (ex. friendly competition to see who can get a higher math grade) and negative peer pressure (ex. a group of girls putting pills of unknown origin into another girls drink).

Part A: Stop-Think-Choose Problem Solving
Part B: Peer Pressure: What is it and What to do about it

Related Quote/Literature:

Stand with anybody that stands right. Stand with him while he is right and part with him when he goes wrong.
--Abraham Lincoln

At my school, all the popular kids in my year swear and wear lots of makeup and get into trouble. I used to think to be cool I had to be like them, but you don't! Being cool is about being yourself, being a good friend, standing up for yourself, and not letting other people push you into things."
--Olivia, 12 (www.pbskids.org)

It Doesn't Have to be This Way: A Barrio Story by Luis J. Rodriguez

Comments:
The Stop-Think-Choose traffic light really lends itself to nonverbal and other physical gestures. You can be creative and make it fun. When conducting Part B, be sure to leave ample time for discussion and be prepared to follow up with individuals who may need one on one attention to discuss harmful Negative Peer Pressure situations.

Procedure – Part A: Stop-Think-Choose

Before Part A: Prepare photocopies of the *Stop-Think-Choose* Activity Sheet.

DO: Draw or display a picture of a traffic signal.

SAY: *Who can identify this object?* Traffic Light. *What is it used for?* It keeps drivers from having accidents. It controls the flow of traffic so no one gets hurt. *What does the red light mean?* Stop. *What does the yellow light mean?* Slow down. Check the other traffic. *What does the green light mean?* Go.

SAY: *That's right. A traffic light keeps the drivers from having accidents. It keeps them for reacting poorly and getting injured. The traffic light is a model for good decision making.*

<u>Red means STOP.</u> *Don't say anything. Don't do anything. Give yourself time to think.*
<u>Yellow means THINK.</u> *Think about your choices. What are your options? Think about the consequences. What will happen after your choice?*
<u>Green means CHOOSE.</u> *Act out your positive choice. Think about the outcome. Was it ethical, fair and just?*

SAY: *Who knows what a consequence is?* It is what happens after your choice. *Can consequences be positive, negative or both?* Both.

DO: Brainstorm a list of Positive Choices and resulting Positive Consequences. Do the same for Negative Choices and Consequences.

DO: Distribute the *Stop-Think-Choose* Activity Sheet. Have students complete on their own.

Procedure – Part B: Peer Pressure

Before Part B: Prepare photocopies of the *What to Do* Activity Sheet and *You Decide...* Activity Sheet. Research newspaper articles or movie clips that show examples of Positive Peer Pressure. Examples may include articles about school fund raising drives or sports teams and the High School Musical movie series. Additionally, many of the television shows on current family or children focused networks have episodes involving peer pressure situations.

SAY: *Peer Pressure is when the people around you try to influence your decision making. It can influence how you dress, the way you act, what you say and what you do for fun.*

Peer Pressure can be POSITIVE and it can be NEGATIVE.

NEGATIVE Peer Pressure happens when others try to get you to say, do or believe things that are not right for you. NEGATIVE Peer Pressure is a problem. POSITIVE Peer Pressure is when others are cheering on your positive and healthy efforts.

SAY: *Have any of you experienced Positive Peer Pressure? How about Negative Peer Pressure? What did you do? What happened during pressure cooker situation? Did you use the STOP-THINK-CHOOSE traffic light? Would you have gotten a different result if you had?* Be sure to validate each response and take time to discuss how the students responded to their previous experiences.

DO: Refer the students to the *What to Do* Activity Sheet. List and define the 5 strategies: Avoid It, Defy It, Alternatives, Stay True, Escape. Set the students in teams of 3 or 4 students per team. Have the teams work as a group to respond to the 3 Negative Peer Pressure scenarios.

DO: After allowing each team to write their responses, assign each of them one of the scenarios for a role play. The teams are to act out the situation with one of students using a strategy to avoid the Negative Peer Pressure.

DO: After each role play discuss how it felt to use one of the strategies. Congratulate each team on their efforts to make healthy decisions and avoid Negative Peer Pressure.

Stop – Think - Choose

Name:_____

STOP
- Don't say anything!
- Don't do anything!
- Give yourself time to think!

THINK
- Think about your choices. What are your options?
- Think about the consequences. What will happen after your choice?

CHOOSE
- Act out your positive choice.
- Think about outcome. Was it fair, ethical and just?

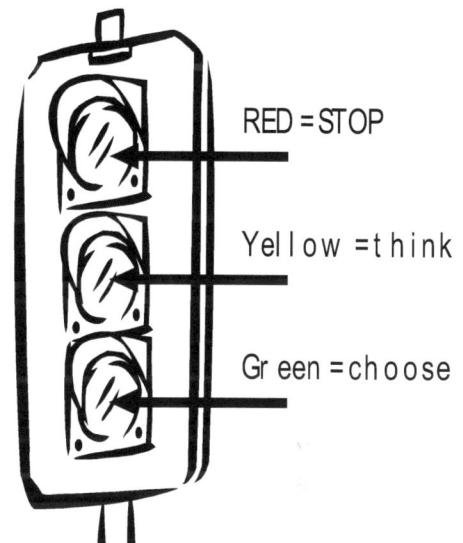

RED = STOP

Yellow = think

Green = choose

CONSEQUENCES are the RESULT of your ACTIONS.

Studying for a test	Making a good grade
Smoking a cigarette	Choking and getting sick
Smiling and being nice	
Doing your chores	
Eating cookies before dinner	
Stealing from your parents	
Skipping breakfast before school	
Staying up late on a school night	
Doing your homework	

What to DO
About Negative Peer Pressure

Peer Pressure is when the people around you try to influence your decision making. It can influence how you dress, the way you act, what you say and what you do for fun.

Peer Pressure can be POSITIVE and it can be NEGATIVE.

NEGATIVE Peer Pressure happens when others try to get you to say, do or believe things that are not right for you.

NEGATIVE Peer Pressure is a problem.

You Don't Have to Accept Negative Peer Pressure

Avoid It	*Choose your friends wisely* *Stay away from pressure cooker situations*
Defy It	*Know that you can say NO* *Sometimes it's OK to not be nice*
Alternatives	*Make excuses to avoid the pressure* *Offer other better ideas or activities*
Stay True	*Stay true to your heart* *Decide what is right for you*
Escape	*If you're being pressured, Leave!* *Don't hang around in the situation*

You Decide...

Name:_____

You decide which strategy to use to overcome Negative Peer Pressure. Write what you would do in the space provided.

Avoid It | Deny It | Alternatives | Stay True | Escape

You are walking home from school with your friends as usual. Today, Bill suggests that you stop in the convenience store for a cold drink. Once inside, Sheila tells you to put 3 candy bars under your shirt and take them without paying.

What do you do? You decide...

You ask the new girl in class to sit with you at lunchtime. Sheila and Bill call her a "freak" and say you can't be their friend and her friend at the same time. They go on to tell you not to sit with her.

What do you do? You decide...

You're playing video games at Bill's house. He puts in a game with a Mature Rating. You know your parents don't allow you to play games with that rating.

What do you do? You decide...

This page intentionally left blank.

Lesson:

#12 Future Planning

Section:

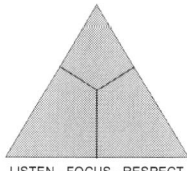
LISTEN - FOCUS - RESPECT

Overview:
The current direction in education has an emphasis on academic outcomes, proficiency targets, graduation rates and college-career readiness. A wide body of research indicates that in order to reach these targets students need to feel meaningful academic and social connections or relationships. In other words students need to experience the relevance of a rigorous curriculum, and feel the warmth and welcome of the positive school climate that is created by caring adults.

Furthermore, students need to learn about the skills and qualities that lie at the heart of successful job performance (SCANS Report for America 2000, College Board Advocacy and Policy Center). These skills, attitudes and beliefs are formed early life, often in the school setting, and have a significant impact on future life-career success.

Beat for Peace seeks to develop attitudes, skills and behaviors that support a positive work ethic leading to school and career success. Use this lesson to connect the dots. By the end be sure that your students understand the connection between the previous lessons and future success in middle school, high school, and/or post secondary education or employment.

Links:
LISTEN/FOCUS/RESPECT –
In the year 2000 the Secretary of Labor issues a report of SCANS skills based on interviews with business leaders around the country. The report found Five Competencies and a Three Part Foundation that are necessary for career success.
SCANS Skills: Listening, Speaking, Creative Thinking, Decision Making, Problem Solving, Knowing How to Learn, Responsibility, Self-Esteem, Self-Management, Sociability, and Honesty.

RESILIENCY SKILL DEVELOPMENT –
The correlation of SCANS skills and the characteristic of resilient children is striking. Both report on the attitudes, skills and beliefs that create intrinsically motivated, resilient and reliable adults.

Materials:
The Future is Up to You Activity Sheet
Graph It! Activity Sheet
Who Would You Hire? Activity Sheet
Internet based career development information available at sites like
www.collegeboard.com, www.careerkey.org, www.careerclusters.org or
www.bls.gov/k12
Paws in Jobland, a web based career exploration program is available at
www.bridges.com

Procedure:
Before the session: Career development information can be challenging for elementary school aged children. Be sure to research age appropriate materials for use in this lesson. The websites listed about are a good place to start. You may also be able to find local support through groups like your state level career development associations, the Chamber of Commerce or the WorkForce Alliance.

DO: Copy and distribute *The Future is Up to You* Activity Sheet. Describe each of the 12 education-career clusters adapted from the Bureau of Labor Statistics website (www.bls.gov/k12).

SAY: *Think about your own likes and dislikes as I describe 12 career interest clusters from the United States Bureau of Labor Statistics. As I read each one rate how much you like those types of things with 1 being not at all and 10 being very interested.*

DO: After the students complete the ratings, instruct them to create a bar graph of their results on the *Graph It!* Activity Sheet. Discuss the results. Be sure to point out how people can be unique in some of their interests and have other areas in common with peers.

SAY: *Now that you have thought about what interests you, let's discuss your skills, attitudes and habits. A skill is something that you are good at. An attitude is a state of mind or feeling. A habit is a behavior that we do almost automatically.* Refer the students the chart on *The Future is Up to You* Activity Sheet. Ask students to report on their own skills, attitudes and habits.

DO: Ask student to share their results. This can be a sensitive topic. Students should offer only positive comments toward their peers. Be ready to deflect any negative comments. Offer encouragement to those willing to share.

SAY: *Do your skills, attitudes and habits help you to be successful? at home? in school? with your friends? How?*

Related Quote/Literature:

You can become the adult you want to be.
--Maria Montessori

We cannot do anything about yesterday, but tomorrow is ours to win or lose.
--Lyndon Baines Johnson

The self is not something that one finds. It's something one creates.
- Thomas Szasz

The 7 Habits of Highly Effective Teens by Sean Covey

What Work Requires of Schools a SCANS Report for America 2000 available at http://wdr.doleta.gov/SCANS

website: You Can Go at http://youcango.collegeboard.org

Comments:

The implications of this lesson can be huge! Once we have convinced our students that they can learn, that what they are learning is relevant, and that by developing good work skills, attitudes and beliefs paths to opportunity will open before them. This is a great lesson to implement and talk about several times a year.

Optional Procedure:

Another way to approach to this lesson is through the use of children's books. Research various children's books that have a clearly identified main character with exaggerated characteristics. Classify each character's attitudes, skills and behaviors as supportive a positive work ethic or as a negative work ethic.

For example, the Cat in the Cat in the Hat by Dr. Seuss is a very extroverted character. His flamboyant attitude and behavior creates all sorts of problems for the children in the story.

SAY: *How do you think the Cat would do in school? Would he be disruptive to your classroom? Why or Why Not? If you owned your own business, would you hire the Cat to work for you? What kind of career would be a good fit for the Cat in the Hat?*

On the other hand, how about Horton in Horton Hears a Who? also by Dr. Seuss? Horton is a very humble, yet conscientious character. Horton's ability to listen carefully results in the saving the entire city of Who-ville.

SAY: *How do you think Horton would do in school? Would he be disruptive to your classroom? Why or Why Not? If you owned your own business, would you hire Horton to work for you?*

DO: Create a T-Chart like and brainstorm a list of qualities or characteristics for each character. Distribute the *Who Would You Hire?* Activity Sheet. Have the students fill in the T-Chart and complete the sheet.

The Future is Up to You

Name:_____

What do You Like?
On a scale of 1 – 10, rate how interested you are in each area.

Not Interested	1	2	3	4	5	6	7	8	9	10	Very Interested

Rating	Education \ Career Area	Rating	Education \ Career Area
	Reading		Sports
	Math		Law Enforcement
	Helping People		Social Studies
	Science		Managing Money
	Building and Fixing Things		Nature
	Music and Art		Computers

What are your skills?
What kind of attitudes do you have?
What are your habits?

Skills	Attitudes	Habits
I am good at math.	*I have a good sense of humor.*	*I do my homework before watching TV.*

Do your Skills, Attitudes and Habits help you to be successful in school or do they pose barriers to your success?

Graph It!

Create a Bar Graph based on your answers.

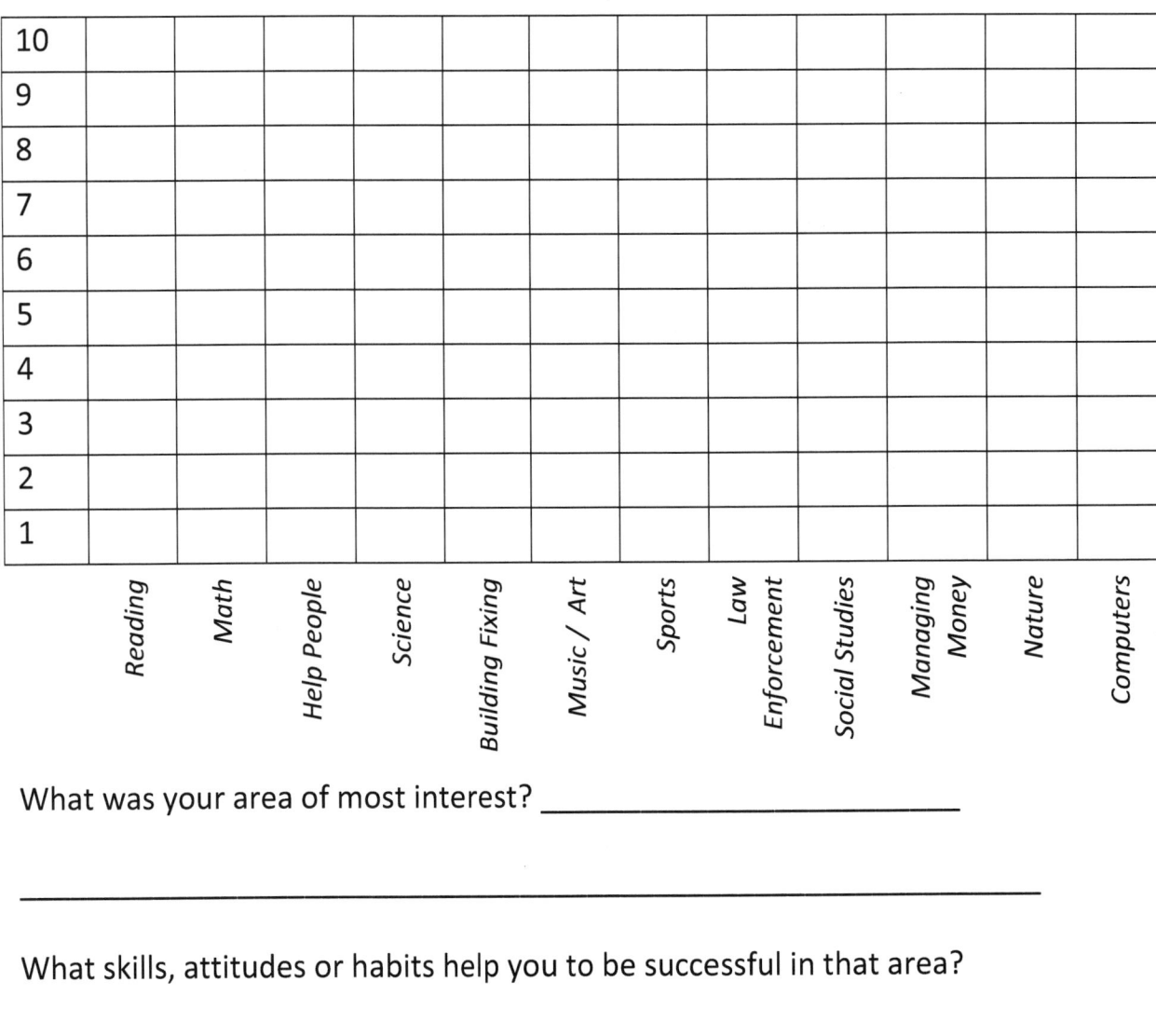

What was your area of most interest? _____

_____

What skills, attitudes or habits help you to be successful in that area?

_____

_____

_____

Who Would You Hire?

Name:_____

Brainstorm and list the qualities of each of Dr. Seuss character.

The Cat in the Hat *from the Cat in the Hat*	Horton *from Horton Hears a Who*

Circle the qualities that would make that character a good friend, successful student, and/or a successful worker.

Which qualities also describe you? List them below:

_____

_____

_____

This page intentionally left blank.

Lesson:

#13 Moving On

Section:

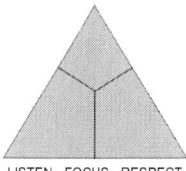

Overview:

The Moving On lesson is like a ceremony in which students and teachers share in their experiences and successes for the year. It provides the chance to recap and bring closure. It is important to remember that the drum ensemble has been a big part of your students' and its ending deserves to be handled appropriately. This is a great opportunity to provide certificates or awards, copies of photographic prints, or to show video of previous performances.

Links:

MUSIC –

If you have any recording of your group's performances, have them ready to play. Also, consider setting up your ensemble to jam your group's favorite songs one last time.

LISTEN/FOCUS/RESPECT –

Ask the questions: *What did you learn a part of the drum ensemble? What did you like the best? What did you like the least?* Students will come back to Listen-Focus-Respect as what they learned. Discuss how these skills, attitudes and beliefs apply in the real life setting.

RESILIENCY SKILL DEVELOPMENT –

As the school year comes to an end students can continue to feel connected. Stress to your students that they will always have a connection to the drum ensemble. Consider inviting them back as alumni. Praise and celebrate the individual and group successes within the drum ensemble and larger school setting. When students feel connected to a caring adult and the school center they become more resilient. When their accomplishments are celebrated their self-efficacy improves and future successes will be more frequent.

Materials:
Certificates or awards
Copies of photographic prints, enough for each student
Audio or video recordings
Student Post Survey

Procedure:
Before the session: Compile arts and crafts supplies (foam picture frames), permanent markers, photographs, and the audio or video recordings. This is also a great time to conduct the *Student Post Survey*.

SAY: *Welcome to our last rehearsal. We have had a fantastic year together. I need to ask you several questions so that we can improve the drum ensemble for next year.*

DO: Distribute and administer the *Student Post Survey*. If appropriate read each item.

SAY: *What did you learn this year in the drum ensemble? How did what you learned help in class? What was your favorite part? What do you think could be improved?* Continue with a discussion like this until everyone has had the opportunity to contribute.

DO: Distribute photos and foam picture frames. Each student should have a photo of him/herself form the previous year's drumming. Make and decorate picture frames as a keepsake.

Optional – Students enjoy being able to autograph each other's shirts. This can become a keepsake, and students like to see themselves represented on each other's shirt.

DO: Listen or play the audio or video recording.

SAY: *How did you feel watching the video?* Elicit various comments. Be sure to focus on the positive comments such as "We were great" or "I felt good playing."

Related Quote/Literature:
Don't cry because it's over. Smile because it happened.
--Dr. Seuss

Comments:
The procedure listed above is what we do at the end of our school year. Your Moving On ceremonies do not have to be the same. Adapt this lesson to meet the individual need and character of your school or drum ensemble.

Beat for Peace Family

Drumming Up Parent Involvement

This page intentionally left blank.

Using Drum Circles for Parent Education

- Drumming is inclusive, nonthreatening and just plain fun. Sale your parent event as a chance to come have fun.

- Build rapport. Many are intimidated by the building. Parents need to feel welcome at school.

- Assess your population's ability to attend school functions. Are mornings best? If the event is at night, what time works best?

- Open the event to school aged children and their little brothers and sisters. Lack of child care may prevent parents from attending.

- Food. Food. Food.

- Use the opportunity to build phone and email lists.

- Schedule events well in advance. Last minute events disrupt work schedules.

- Offer specific invitations to your male figures (dads, uncles, grandfather, etc) too.

This page intentionally left blank.

Parent Lesson: **Section:**

#1 Listening Skills in the Family

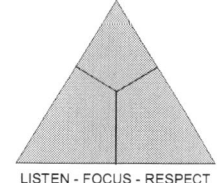

Overview:

- Define active listening as listening to the sound, the content, and feeling in communication.
- Define communication as speaking (sending a clear message) and listening (receiving and understanding the message).
- Define paraphrasing as restating the sender's message with an understanding of content and feeling.
- Learn active listing and paraphrasing skills.
- Familiarize the participants with the drum circle.
- Demonstrate the oral-aural tradition using call-response and echo patterns.
- Link the drum ensemble activity to listening skills.

Materials:

- *Communication Diagram* Activity Sheet
- *SLANT* Activity Sheet
- *Roadblocks* to Good Communication Activity Sheet
- *Paraphrasing* Activity Sheet
- World Music Drumming: A Cross Cultural Curriculum
- Tubanos, shakaree, cowbell, gankogui as appropriate for the participants, set in a circle.

Procedure:

1. Welcome and thank the participants for giving up their valuable time tonight. *You are here because you want the best for your children and your family.*

2. Discuss the current level of listening in their homes. *Is anyone frustrated with the quality of listening at home?* Contrast active listening with hearing. *Active listening requires getting past the video games, music players, and "yes, dears."*

3. Orient participants to their instruments and demonstrate the sounds that each makes.

4. Play echo patterns. Discuss what one has to do in order to be successful (**Listen-Focus-Respect**). Discuss how important it is to play exactly what the leader plays. *Remember children are like sponges. They say what we say. Talk the way we talk. Act the way we act.*

5. Introduce call-response and call-response-echo using "What's your name?" Discuss the importance of playing what the other person played not what you think they should have played.

6. Display the SLANT Activity Sheet. Discuss the skills of a good listener.

7. Display the *Roadblocks to Good Communication* Activity Sheet. Ask *What happens when we have miscommunication? Have you ever suffered from miscommunication with someone else? What was the consequence?* Be prepared with anecdotes from your own life experiences.

8. Display *Paraphrasing* Activity Sheet. Conduct a 60 second report in which participants partner up and speak on a subject for 60 seconds. Good subjects include favorite movie, if I had a million dollars, coolest dream, best vacation and so on. The listener must actively listen for content and feeling and then paraphrase it back.

SAY: *Active listening is hard work!* Congratulate them on their effort. *What do you already do well? What would you like to get better at? What can you take from tonight to try this week?*

Related Quote/Literature:

Watch your thoughts, they become words.
Watch your words, they become actions.
Watch your actions, they become habits.
Watch your habits, they become character.
Watch your character, it becomes your destiny.
-- John Outlaw

THE 3 INGREDIENTS FOR EFFECTIVE COMMUNICATION

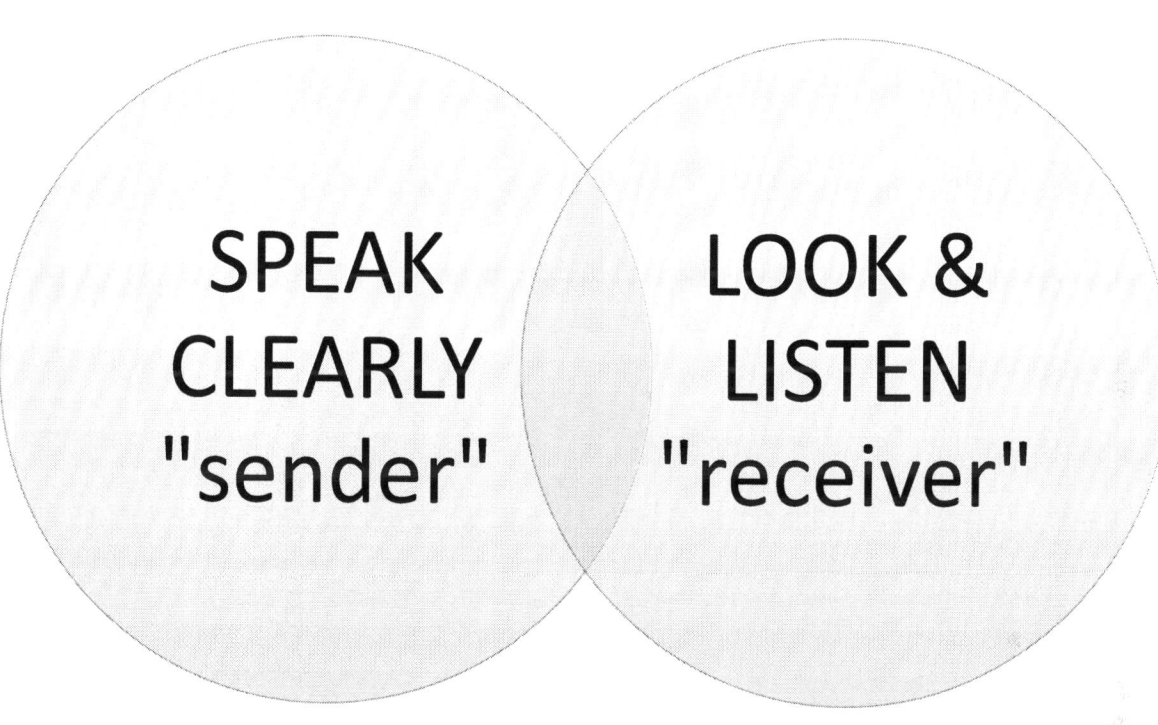

SLANT

Sit Still

Look at the speaker

Ask questions

Nod your head

Think about what is being said

ROADBLOCKS

	Mumbling Fuzzy Messages Tone of Voice Not Giving Details
Not Asking Questions Hearing, NOT Listening Strong Emotions Being Distracted	

Roadblocks disrupt the *sending* and *receiving* of <u>important</u> messages and often results in conflict.

Paraphrasing

not just being a copycat

You said _____

You feel_____

Because_____

(and you want me to _____)

When paraphrasing be sure to pay attention to the *feeling*. You don't have to be 100% correct in guessing the other person's feeling. The value is in building the *empathy bridge*.

Parent Lesson: **Section:**

#2 Communication and I-Messages in the Family

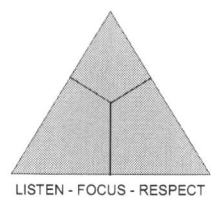
LISTEN - FOCUS - RESPECT

Overview:

- Define communication as speaking (sending a clear message), listening (receiving the message), and understanding the message.
- Define I-Messages as a non threatening way of sending a variety of corrective and non-corrective messages. Define You-messages as threatening and intimidating.
- Develop skill with I-messages.
- Familiarize the participants with the drum circle.
- Demonstrate the oral-aural tradition using call-response and echo patterns.
- Demonstrate and play complimentary rhythms. Discuss how complimentary rhythms should make sense and add to the existing musical conversation.

Materials:

- *Communication Diagram* Activity Sheet
- *Non-Verbal Communication Cards* Activity Sheet
- *I-Messages* Activity Sheet
- World Music Drumming: A Cross Cultural Curriculum
- Tubanos, shakaree, cowbell, gankogui as appropriate for the participants, set in a circle

Procedure:

1. Welcome and thank the participants for giving up their valuable time tonight. Display and review the *Communication Diagram* Activity Sheet.

2. Discuss the qualities of a "You message". *You did this…You did that…* What feelings and thoughts do we have when a conversation starts with the word "you"? Attacked? Cornered?

3. Discuss how the manner and tone in which we send a message is as important as the content of the message. Half of communication is sending messages through non-verbal means. Display *Non-Verbal Communication Cards* Activity Sheet. Have volunteers pantomime the examples of non-verbal communication.

4. Play echo patterns. Discuss what one has to do in order to be successful. *Non-verbal messages rely on the eyes to see the other persons body language and facial expressions.* Play echo pattern again, this time have participants close their eyes. *Did not being able to see make it easier or more difficult to repeat my message?*

5. Display the *I-Messages* Activity Sheet. Practice I-Messages in pairs using pretend scenarios. For example, "your son left his new bike outside in the rain", "your friend yelled at you over a video game", or "your mother embarrasses you in front of your friends by tickling your chin".

6. Start complimentary rhythms and have the participants join in. Note how we must listen to what is being said (played) in order to join into the conversation groove) in a way that makes sense. Our part should not be overbearing or abusive.

SAY: *Communication is hard work! I-messages can field weird.* Congratulate them on their effort. *Would you rather receive an I-message or a You-message?*

SAY: *What do you already do well? What would you like to get better at? What can you take from tonight to try this week?*

Related Quote/Literature:

My childhood should have taught me lessons for my own fatherhood, but it didn't because parenting can only be learned by people who have no children.
--Bill Cosby

Non Verbal Communication

- How you say something matters as much as what you say.

- You can say a lot without speaking.

- Body language is important.

- Facial expressions give hints as to how you really think or feel.

How would you use nonverbal Communication to "say" the following?

Hello.	Goodbye
I am frustrated.	I'm bored.
Come here.	I Won!
I don't care what you say!	I feel scared.
Disgusting!	I feel happy.

Non Verbal Communication Cards

I am happy	I am sad
I am angry	I am embarrassed
Come here	Stop
I won!	What's up?
I'm confused	Who cares?
I'm OK	He quiet
Leave me alone	I am lonely
_____	_____

I - Messages

I feel _____,

When you _____,

Because _____,

I want _____.

What if your daughter left her bike in the front yard in the rain?

I feel *frustrated*,

When you leave *your bike outside in the rain*,

Because *it cost a lot of money*,

I want *you to take better care of your bike and put it into the garage*.

You try it...

Your Mom shows your baby pictures to your friends.

Your son does not put up the tools and leaves them a mess.

I feel _____,

When you _____,

Because _____,

I want _____.

This page intentionally left blank.

Parent Lesson: **Section:**

#3 Responsibility in the Family

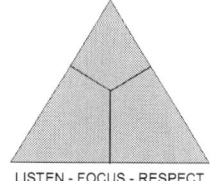

Overview:

- Define responsibility as doing what you are supposed to do and accepting the consequences of your actions.
- List common responsibilities for children and adults.
- Familiarize the participants with the drum circle.
- Demonstrate the oral-aural tradition using call-response and echo patterns.
- Learn and play Ensemble 1. Discuss how each section is responsible for its own little part in the ensemble.

Materials:

- World Music Drumming: A Cross Cultural Curriculum - Ensemble 1
- *Family Responsibilities* T-Chart
- Tubanos, shakaree, cowbell, gankogui as appropriate for the participants, set in a circle.

Procedure:

1. Welcome and thank the participants for giving up their valuable time tonight.

2. Teach Ensemble 1. Discuss the difficulty level of each part.

3. Combine all of the Ensemble 1 parts. Discuss how when played alone each part is simple. When combined the parts become more intricate and exciting.

4. Define and discuss how each drummer has a responsibility to the ensemble. When we play together we make music. Discuss what would happen if someone skipped their responsibilities. Discuss how that works with families. *Families work together. We each have our own role and each person's role should complement the other. Sometimes a family member gets off track. The family can help and encourage each other.*

5. Use a T-Chart to brainstorm how to encourage responsibility in the home.
- clearly define adult-child roles
- be regular and consistent with home schedule
- list and assign chores to family members
- allow positive and negative consequences to occur unless the result would be injurious
- be a role model
- offer choices within limits that you find acceptable

SAY: *We all want our child to be responsible. Trickle it in through daily modeling and teaching of the attitude, skills and belief of responsible behavior.*

SAY: *What do you already do well? What would you like to get better at? What can you take from tonight to try this week?*

Related Quote/Literature:

You know the only people who are always sure about the proper way to raise children? Those who've never had any.
--Bill Cosby

Family Responsibilities

Parent Responsibilities	Child Responsibilities

What do you notice when you compare both sides of the chart?

_____

_____

This page intentionally left blank.

Parent Lesson: **Section:**

#4
Teamwork
in the Family

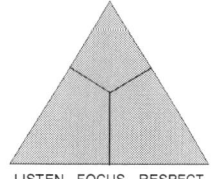

Overview:

- Define teamwork as cooperation as "to do together". Community is the benefactor of teamwork.
- Review/discuss the responsibility of playing your part in ensemble 1.
- List ways that athletic teams, communities and families display teamwork
- Learn *Harambee* (World Music Drumming: New Ensembles and Songs). Discuss how the ensemble is about "pulling together" and teamwork.

Materials:

- Chart paper.
- World Music Drumming: A Cross Cultural Curriculum – *Harambee*
- Tubanos, shakaree, cowbell, gankogui as appropriate for the participants, set in a circle.

Procedure:

1. Welcome and thank the participants for giving up their valuable time tonight.

2. *Harambee* literally means "all pull together". Discuss the definition of teamwork as working together towards a common goal. Team work can be considered to have two complementary elements:
   - Divide and conquer is when tasks are divided and the individual completes the task.
   - Bucket brigade is when two or more individuals cooperate on the same task.

Discuss benefits of teamwork. Brainstorm examples of teamwork.

3. Teach *Harambee*. Add the lyrics. Ask the group to work together by encouraging each other and providing assistance.

4. Discuss how to encourage teamwork at home:
- have children help with grocery shopping,
- work together to fold laundry,
- have older children help with oil changes and other vehicle maintenance,
- chore responsibilities,
- family meetings with all persons participating,
- read stories about characters working together, or
- plan recreation and/or trips together

SAY: *Teamwork is hard work! Coach and encourage your children to work together.*

SAY: *What do you already do well? What would you like to get better at? What can you take from tonight to try this week?*

Related Quote/Literature:

Individually, we are one drop. Together, we are an ocean.
--Ryunosuke Satoro

Parent Lesson: **Section:**

#5 Listen-Focus-Respect in the Family

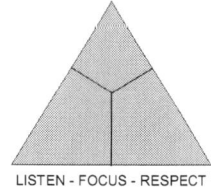

Overview:

- Learn **Listen-Focus-Respect** guidelines for home.
- Review definition for listening.
- Define Respect as treating the other the way you want to be treated.
- Define Focus as paying attention to what is important at any given point in time. Focus can shift from situation to situation.
- Understand how caring and respect helps to connect individuals with their family and community.
- Familiarize the participants with the drum circle.
- Demonstrate the oral-aural tradition using call-response, call-response-echo and echo patterns.

Materials:

- Chart paper.
- *Listen-Focus-Respect Make it Real!* Activity Sheet.
- World Music Drumming: A Cross Cultural Curriculum
- Tubanos, shakaree, cowbell, gankogui as appropriate for the participants, set in a circle.

Procedure:

1. Welcome and thank the participants for giving up their valuable time tonight.

2. Play question-answer patterns such as *What's your name?*, which requires participants to sound out their name on the drum. Or, *What's for dinner?*, which requires participants to play what they plan to have for dinner on their drum. Once you have this down, add in an echo element. The question-answer-echo activity requires everyone to listen to and then copy the answer. It goes something like this: (Q) *What's your name?* (A) *MIKE*. (EQ) *What's his name?* (E) *MIKE*; (Q) *What's your name?* (A) *CATHY*. (EQ) *What's her name?* (E) *CATHY*. Discuss how we demonstrate respect and caring by playing the person's name correctly.

4. Discuss and chart how we model **Listen**
   - Listen and make eye contact.
   - Make time to listen – not while driving or making dinner.
   - Say "This is important, I need you to really listen."

5. Discuss and chart how we model **Focus**
   - Set and keep family goals.
   - Pay attention to tasks at hand. Explain why it is important to focus. For example, while using power tools, be focused or you could get injured.

6. Discuss and chart how we model **Respect**
   - Knock before entering your child's room.
   - Use language, words and tone of voice that would be acceptable to you.
   - Give your child space and allow for their opinions.
   - Correct your child discretely and without sarcasm.
   - Let your child answer questions for him\herself.

7. Display and Discuss the ***Listen-Focus-Respect** Make it Real!* Activity Sheet.

SAY: *Caring and respect are dispositions that can be attenuated through skill building. How does an I-message demonstrate respect? What communication skill demonstrates respect?*

SAY: *What do you already do well? What would you like to get better at? What can you take from tonight to try this week?*

Related Quote/Literature:

A tree is known by its fruit.
--Proverb Quote

The apple doesn't fall far from the tree.
--unknown

Listen-Focus-Respect
Make it Real!

	Show	Tell	Do	Independence	Connect
Listen	• Make Time • Active Listening • Eye Contact • Nonverbal and Verbal Encouragement	• Describes the SLANT Steps to Listening • Play Listening Games • Read • Paraphrase	• Play Listening Games • Ask for Active Listening • Offer Active Listening • Connect and Communicate	• Recognize and Praise Listening • Ask him/her to Teach it to Others	• Associate Listening to school, social, familial, and career success.
Focus	• Eye Contact • Set Family Routines • Set Family Goals and Priorities • Value Relationships	• Hold Family Meetings • Talk About Priorities and Goals	• Allow Children to Contribute • Adhere to Family and Homework Routines	• Allow Children to Develop Interests and Activities	• Associate Focus to school, social, familial, and career success.
Respect	• Respect Yourself • Say What You Mean. Mean What you Say • Set Limits • Use Respectful Language	• Set Limits • Describe Respectful Language • Discuss Respect for Self and Others	• Use Respectful Language Everyday • Maintain Healthy Habits • Adhere to Limits	• Make Children Responsible for Self Care • Allow for appropriate Decision Making Opportunities	• Associate Respect to school, social, familial, and career success.

This page intentionally left blank.

Parent Lesson: **Section:**

#6 Balance in the Family

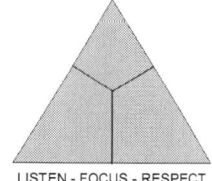
LISTEN - FOCUS - RESPECT

Overview:

- Define wellness as establishing an overall quality of life in the family.
- Wellness is about striking a balance between work, leisure, and family.
- Define the three ingredients to family wellness; Relax, Fun, and Time.
- Drumming for wellness is about feeling as good as one possibly can – reducing the impact of everyday stressors.
- Learn Ensemble 2 - *Take Time in Life* World Music Drumming: A Cross Cultural Curriculum
- Familiarize the participants with the drum circle.
- Demonstrate the oral-aural tradition using call-response and echo patterns.

Materials:

- *Take Time in Life* - World Music Drumming: A Cross Cultural Curriculum
- Chart paper.
- Sleeve of small plastic or Styrofoam cups.
- Tubanos, shakaree, cowbell, gankogui as appropriate for the audience, set in a circle.

Procedure:

1. Welcome and thank the participants for giving up their valuable time tonight.

2. Divide the group into 5 subgroups: bell, shaker, low drum, medium drum and high drum. Play complementary rhythms like those in ensemble 1. Discuss musical balance in the drum circle. *What would happen if we allowed one part to dominate? What happens if one part of our life dominates?*

3. Call for one volunteer to symbolize our "daily grind". Brainstorm and record on chart paper all of the little stressors that occur during our daily lives. For each example, give the volunteer one cup to hold. Eventually he/she will lose balance and drop the cups. Discuss how the cups represent when we try to juggle too many tasks.

4. Discuss strategies to minimize stress events
   - Make Relaxation a priority
   - Make Time with family a priority.
   - Make Fun a priority.
   - say no!
   - allow extra time for travel
   - set up a daily routine
   - reward yourself
   - stress reduction techniques
   - deep breathing
   - muscle relaxation
   - Take Time in Life

5. Learn ensemble 2 and *Take Time in Life*. Add in the lyrics.

ASK: *What do the lyrics mean to you?*

6. Praise the family's commitment to take time with one another in the drum circle.

Related Quote/Literature:

The time to relax is when you don't have time for it.
--Sidney J. Harris

A happy family is but an earlier heaven.
-- John Bowring

Beat for Peace

Forms and Tools

The original purchaser of this book can request an electronic copy of the forms and tools used throughout the *Talking Drum: A Beat for Peace Curriculum*.

The electronic copy may be printed for instructional use in one school only. Any other use is strictly prohibited.

To request your electronic copy of the forms and tools, email Michael C. Kane directly at Mike@BeatforPeace.com.

DRUM ENSEMBLE STUDENT REFERRAL FORM

Your teachers and school staff can be your greatest ally when developing a drum ensemble intervention. Remember that you are asking to work with those students who are exhibiting the least amount of motivation and the greatest deal of academic and behavior difficulty out of the entire class. Your teachers and staff will be appreciative of your efforts. The following referral form is a great way to introduce your staff to the program by outlining the criteria for participation (presence of risk factors). It also allows them to refer specific students based on their observations.

This page intentionally left blank.

Drum Ensemble
Student Referral Form

Referring Teacher/Staff/Adult Name:_____

The promotion of protective factors as a way to mitigate risk is achieved through the use of a world music style drum ensemble. Along with musical rhythms, students learn the traits of social competence, school affiliation, positive self-concept, a sense of purpose and future, and the value of diversity. All of this occurs within an environment rich in caring, support, high expectations and meaningful participation. The Drum Ensemble is based on resiliency research and the World Music Drumming (Will Schmid, 1998) curriculum.

Students are selected based on the presence of multiple risk factors such as:

Individual/ Peer	Alienation/Rebelliousness Friends who engage in problem behavior Favorable attitudes toward problem behavior
Family	Family management problems Family conflict Family history of problem behavior
School	Early academic failure Early conduct problems Lack of commitment to school/poor affiliation
Community	Availability of drugs and/or weapons Community laws and norms favorable toward problem behavior Low neighborhood attachment and community disorganization Severe economic deprivation

Adapted from Adler & Smith (1998). <u>*School Staff Guide to Risk and Resiliency*</u>

Use the space below to list the names of any fourth and fifth grade student(s) you feel are living in the presence of multiple risk factors and who may also benefit from this intervention.

Student Name	Teacher Name	Risk Factors/Comments

The drum ensemble is a student intervention in which participants are held accountable in the areas of academic performance, daily attendance, and appropriate behavior. In addition, students' classroom focus, social competence and participation are rated by their teachers throughout the year. Even though we do not expect perfection right away, we do expect effective effort and celebrate incremental gains.

DRUM ENSEMBLE PERMISSION SLIP

In addition to any school or district required permission forms, I recommend that the following be completed. Again, it provides information in addition to obtaining consent. You will notice the portion that addresses being photographed. Including this will help address issues that may arise from being photographed by the press or other legitimately interested parties.

This page intentionally left blank.

Drum Ensemble

PERMISSION SLIP

Date: _____,

Your child, _____, is being provided the opportunity to participate in an exciting school Drum Ensemble. The Drum Ensemble uses a world music drum ensemble to build school success skills such as (but not limited to) demonstrating respect, focus, listening, and responsibility. Our ability to use musical rhythms while building these skills makes this a very popular performing group.

There are four integral parts to the Drum Ensemble program. Students attend weekly drum ensemble rehearsals. Twice a month students will meet with the school counselor during the school day to discuss their school successes. Throughout the year after school performances will be scheduled. Finally, Drum Ensemble participants are expected to maintain appropriate academic focus and behavior at all times.

For more information please call _____.

See attached permission slip.

Drum Ensemble

PERMISSION SLIP

My child, _____, may participate in the drum ensemble. My child may participate in the twice-monthly group sessions with the school counselor.

_____   _____
Parent Name   Parent Signature

Due to the popularity of the Drum Ensemble, we are often photographed.

_____ My child may be photographed.

_____ My child may not be photographed. Every reasonable effort will be taken to prevent photographs from being taken.

_____   _____
Parent Name   Parent Signature

DRUM ENSEMBLE COMPACT

From day one we discuss what it means to make a commitment. Making a commitment to the drum ensemble means that all persons agree to **Listen**, **Focus** and **Respect** one another. Furthermore, students now represent the larger group in class and around campus. A signed agreement listing specific expectations shows that we mean business.

This page intentionally left blank.

Drum Ensemble Compact

As a proud member of the **Drum Ensemble**, I agree to:

Listen:

- Look at my teacher and any adult when they are speaking.
- Wait for my turn or permission before speaking.
- Follow my teacher's or any adult's direction first time given.
- Ask questions when I do not understand what I have heard.
- Hear the sound and silence the drum ensemble makes when we play.

Focus:

- Look at my teacher and any adult when they are speaking.
- Complete work assignments immediately.
- Understand what is being said.
- Avoid being distracted by things that matter least.
- Understand the meaning behind the drum ensemble.

Respect:

- Look at my teacher and any adult when they are speaking.
- Use manner words when talking with others.
- Use careful actions with others inside and outside the drum ensemble.
- Come to the drum ensemble with care and ready to play.

_____ _____ _____ _____
Drum Ensemble Member   Date   Classroom Teacher   Date

_____ _____ _____ _____
Name/Position   Date   Name/Position   Date

This page intentionally left blank.

HELLO BONGO

This spin off of a widely available activity is used during the first drum ensemble session. The *World Music Drumming* (Will Schmid, 1998) curriculum lists other first session activities, such as "what's your name". These activities are a great way to break the ice and to get students interacting with one another.

This page intentionally left blank.

Hello Bongo!

Step 1: Find someone who fits the description listed below.
Step 2: Face the other person and say "Hello, my name is____, what is your name?"
Step 3: Write their name in the box.

Someone who has been to Walt Disney World.	Someone born the same month as you.	Someone who wears glasses.	Someone who likes mushrooms on their pizza.
Someone who has (or had) the same teacher as you.	Someone who knows how to spell responsibility.	Someone with the same hair color as you.	Someone with the same favorite food as you.
Someone who made an A or B on their last school test.	Someone who was in the Drum Circle last year.	Someone with the same number of family members as you.	Someone who knows the motto of the Drum Circle.

This page intentionally left blank.

STUDENT PRE-SURVEY

The Student Pre-Survey should be administered during the first month of the intervention. The Pre-Survey will provide baseline data for comparison once the post survey is administered. The Pre-Survey was written to rate the student's perception of him/herself in terms of the characteristics of a resilient child. The survey can also be used to identify data trends that warrant discussion. For example, if a majority of students report that they HARDLY EVER or NEVER stand up for themselves without putting others down (#2), then additional counseling sessions and discussions on assertiveness and I-messages may be appropriate. I recommend the survey items be read to the students to avoid any anxiety about the reading level.

This page intentionally left blank.

Drum Ensemble
Student Pre-Survey

Name: _____ Date: _____

Circle Your Best Answer

5=ALWAYS   4=MOSTLY   3=SOMETIMES   2=HARDLY EVER   1=NEVER

1	I can work with someone who has different opinions than mine.	5	4	3	2	1
2	I can stand up for myself without putting others down.	5	4	3	2	1
3	I can work out my own problems.	5	4	3	2	1
4	I can do most things if I try.	5	4	3	2	1
5	I feel bad when someone gets their feelings hurt.	5	4	3	2	1
6	When I need help, I find someone to talk with.	5	4	3	2	1
7	I can pay attention in class.	5	4	3	2	1
8	I understand my moods and feelings.	5	4	3	2	1
9	I plan to graduate from high school.	5	4	3	2	1
10	At my school, I do important things that make a difference.	5	4	3	2	1
11	I try to work out problems by talking about them.	5	4	3	2	1
12	At my school, teachers and other adults listen when I have something to say.	5	4	3	2	1
13	My friends try to do what is right.	5	4	3	2	1
14	This past year, how many times have you hit or pushed other kids when you were not playing around?	0-1	2-3	4-5	6 or more	
15	This past year, how many times have you spread mean rumors about others kids at school?	0-1	2-3	4-5	6 or more	

16. Our songs are about respect, focus, and hopes and dreams. What are your hopes and dreams for this year?

_____

_____

_____

_____

_____

17. What are your hopes and dreams for the next 5 years? 10 years? What do you see yourself doing with your education or career?

_____

_____

_____

_____

_____

18. This year I want to learn _____

_____

_____

_____

STUDENT POST-SURVEY

The Student Post-Survey should be administered during the last month of the intervention. Compare the responses to the Pre-Survey results. Be sure to look for data trends and adjust the intervention as needed. I recommend the survey items be read to the students to avoid any anxiety about the reading level.

This page intentionally left blank.

Drum Ensemble
Student Post-Survey

Name: _____   Date: _____

Circle Your Best Answer

       5=ALWAYS   4=MOSTLY   3=SOMETIMES   2=HARDLY EVER   1=NEVER

1	I can work with someone who has different opinions than mine.	5	4	3	2	1
2	I can stand up for myself without putting others down.	5	4	3	2	1
3	I can work out my own problems.	5	4	3	2	1
4	I can do most things if I try.	5	4	3	2	1
5	I feel bad when someone gets their feelings hurt.	5	4	3	2	1
6	When I need help, I find someone to talk with.	5	4	3	2	1
7	I can pay attention in class.	5	4	3	2	1
8	I understand my moods and feelings.	5	4	3	2	1
9	I plan to graduate from high school.	5	4	3	2	1
10	At my school, I do important things that make a difference.	5	4	3	2	1
11	I try to work out problems by talking about them.	5	4	3	2	1
12	At my school, teachers and other adults listen when I have something to say.	5	4	3	2	1
13	My friends try to do what is right.	5	4	3	2	1
14	This past year, how many times did you hit or pushed other kids when you were not playing around?	0-1	2-3	4-5	6 or more	
15	This past year, how many times have you spread mean rumors about others kids at school?	0-1	2-3	4-5	6 or more	

19. What did you accomplish or learn as a part of the Drum Ensemble?

_____
_____
_____
_____

20. Did you reach your hopes and dreams for this school year? How?

_____
_____
_____
_____

21. Rate how you feel about your participation in the Drum Ensemble.

(terrible) 1   2   3   4   5   6   7   8   9   10 *(wonderful)*

22. What do you think could make the Drum Ensemble better?

_____
_____
_____
_____

TEACHER RATING SCALE

The Teacher Rating Scale should be administered several times during the intervention period. I recommend an early, middle and end administration. Teachers appreciate the brief nature of the rating scale. Many like to write additional comments. Use this information to identify whole group trends as well as intervention points for specific students.

This page intentionally left blank.

Teacher Rating Scale

Drummer Name:_____ Teacher Name:_____ Date:_____

In an effort to judge the effectiveness of the Drum Ensemble intervention, we will be collecting data on participating students. We truly appreciate your support of our efforts.

Please circle that best describes the student.

5=ALWAYS   4=MOSTLY   3=SOMETIMES   2=HARDLY EVER   1=NEVER

1. Pays attention in class.	5	4	3	2	1
2. Practices good listening habits.	5	4	3	2	1
3. Follows directions.	5	4	3	2	1
4. Works well independently.	5	4	3	2	1
5. Completes assignments on time.	5	4	3	2	1
6. Follows school rules.	5	4	3	2	1
7. Respects other's rights and feelings.	5	4	3	2	1
8. Shows self-confidence.	5	4	3	2	1
9. Recognizes importance of academics.	5	4	3	2	1
10. Shows empathy for others.	5	4	3	2	1
11. Readily offers solutions for difficult social problems.	5	4	3	2	1
12. Recognizes their role in school success.	5	4	3	2	1

This page intentionally left blank.

WEEKLY CHECK-IN SHEET TEACHER RATING SCALE

Many times it is important to gather more frequent, or weekly, data on students. The Weekly Check-In Sheet is completed by the classroom teachers every week. The student drummer is responsible for getting it to and from the teacher every week. The check-in sheet allows the student, teacher and intervention leader to establish a data-feedback loop. Use the data to celebrate small improvements as well to establish short term improvement goals.

This page intentionally left blank.

Drummer Check-In Sheet

Name:_____   Week of:_____

Student Drummers are expected to **Listen**, show **Respect**, and be **Focused** both in the drum circle and in the classroom. Please circle the response their best describes their performance in these areas for this week.

Listen			
Practices good listening habits.	Hardly Ever	Sometimes	Almost Always
Asks questions/ participates.	Hardly Ever	Sometimes	Almost Always

Focus			
Pays attention in class.	Hardly Ever	Sometimes	Almost Always
Completes assignments.	Hardly Ever	Sometimes	Almost Always

Respect			
Follows rule and procedures.	Hardly Ever	Sometimes	Almost Always
Uses caring language and behavior.	Hardly Ever	Sometimes	Almost Always

Teacher Signature_____

Student Strengths this week.

Student Goal for next week.

This page intentionally left blank.

DRUMMER SELF-EVALUATION REPORT

The Drummer Self-Evaluation Report is a very robust and powerful tool when used during small group discussions. Most students are very honest in the self-report. Combine the self-evaluation report with hard data, such as report card grades, standardized test scores, attendance data, and discipline data to generate "right now" goal statements. Goal setting is a very important skill and this document provides significant amounts of information for identifying areas for improvement.

This page intentionally left blank.

Drummer Self-Evaluation Report

Name:_____   Date:_____

Rate yourself 1-5 for each item.

1 – Always   2 – Mostly   3 – Sometimes   4 – Not Often   5 – Never

	I am a good drummer.
	I listen and follow directions in class.
	I focus on my work in class.
	I participate in class.
	I seek help when I am unsure of what to do.
	My behavior is good and shows respect for myself and others.
	I complete my class work and homework on time.
	I come to school everyday.

Write any statements with a score of 3, 4 or 5 below. Use your answers to help make goals for yourself. Your answers will be kept private.

_____

_____

This page intentionally left blank.

GUIDED INTERVIEW: PARENT / TEACHER VERSION

The following Parent and Teacher guided interviews were created with two purposes in mind. Primarily, the interviews were designed to gather important process data about the drum ensemble intervention. By sitting one on one with a parent or teacher I was able to assess some of the more intangible strengths of the intervention. A second and equitably important goal was to show these two major stakeholding groups that I was serious about improving the academic and behavioral functioning of my drummers - their students and children.

This page intentionally left blank.

Drum Ensemble Guided Interview
Parent Version

Interviewer Name:_____   Date:_____

Who is your child?
_____

How old is your child?
_____

How long has your child been in the drum ensemble?
_____

Have you seen your child perform? How did you feel? How do you think your child felt?
_____
_____
_____

Has your child talked to you about the drum ensemble? What topics?
_____
_____
_____

What do you think *"Listen, Focus, Respect"* means?
_____
_____
_____

What impact do you feel that the drum ensemble has had on your child in regards to behavior? Academics? Respect? Responsibility?
_____
_____
_____

Drum Ensemble Guided Interview
Teacher Version

Interviewer Name:_____ Date:_____

Who is your student
_____

How long has your student been in the Drum Ensemble?
_____

Have you seen your student perform? How did you feel? How do you think your student felt?
_____
_____
_____

Has your student talked to you about the Drum Ensemble? What topics?
_____
_____
_____

What do you think *"Listen, Focus, Respect"* means?
_____
_____
_____

What impact do you feel that the Drum Ensemble has had on your student in regards to behavior? Academics? Respect? Responsibility?
_____
_____
_____

Beat for Peace

Research and References

This page intentionally left blank.

Selected References

Adler, A. & Smith J. (1998). School staff guide to risk and resiliency. Florida Department of Education: Tallahassee, FL.

Belli, R (2001). Drumming: The future is in your hands. Teaching Music, Vol 9 Issue 3, 48-52.

Bernard, B. (1991). Fostering resiliency in kids: Protective factors in the family, school, and community. Portland, OR: Western Center for Drug-Free Schools and Communities.

Bernard, B. (1996). The foundations of the resiliency paradigm. Resiliency in Action, Winter, 7-11.

Brigman, G. & Campbell, C. (2003). Helping students improve academic achievement and school success behavior. Professional School Counselor, Vol. 7 Issue 2, 91-98.

Brooks, K. (1997). Too much fun for therapy: Therapeutic recreation as an intervention tool with at-risk youth. A series of Solutions and Strategies, 11, 1-9.

Cesarone, B. (1999). Resilience guide: A collection of resources on resilience on children and families. Illinois: Office of Educational Research and Improvement

Corbiere, P. (2010). Skins, sticks and bars: Percussion ensembles for elementary and middle school. Iowa: Heritage Music Press.

Isaacs, M. (2003). Data driven decision making: The engine of accountability. Professional School Counseling, Vol 6 Issue 4, 288-295.

Kaffenberg, C. & Young, A. (2008). Making data work. Virginia: American School Counselor Association.

Milstein, M. M. & Henry D. A. (2000). Spreading resiliency: Making it happen for schools and communities. California: Corwin Press.

Nash, J. K. & Fraser, M. W. (1998). After-school care for children: A resiliency based approach. The Journal of Contemporary Human Services, July-August, 370-383.

Rak, C. F. & Patterson, L. E. (1996). Promoting resilience in at-risk children. Journal of Counseling & Development, 74, 368-373.

Richardson, G. E. & Nixon, C. J. (1997). A curriculum for resiliency. Principal, 77(2), 26-28.

Schmid, W. (1998). World music drumming: A cross cultural curriculum. Wisconsin: Hall Leonard.

Schmid, W. (2004). World music drumming: New ensembles and songs. Wisconsin: Hall Leonard.

Scott, J. E. (1996). Self-efficacy: A key to literacy learning. Reading Horizons, 36(3), 195-212.

Stevens, C. K., & Burt, J. W. (1997). Drum circles: Theory and application in the mental health treatment continuum. Continuum. 4(2), 175-184.

Stevens, C. (2000) Rainbows of Rhythm: Rebuilding after the storm of Columbine. www.remo.com. Health Rhythms Article 18.

Stone, C. & Dahir, C. (2004) School counselor accountability: A measure of student success. New Jersey: Prentice Hall.

U. S. of Education. (1998). Creative partnerships for prevention: Using the arts and humanities to build resiliency in youth. Washington, DC: Learning Systems Group.

Webb, L., Brigman, G., & Campbell C. (2005). Linking school counselors and student success: A replication of the student success skills approach targeting the academic social competence of students. Professional School Counseling, Vol. 8 Issue 5, 407-413.

Selected Internet Resources

Beat for Peace – www.beatforpeace.com

World Music Drumming www.worldmusicdrumming.com

Remo Drums - www.remo.com

The College Board – www.collegeboard.org

National Office for School Counselor Advocacy - http://advocacy.collegeboard.org

You Can Go! - http://youcango.collegeboard.org

Center for School Counseling Outcome Research & Evaluation – www.umass.edu/schoolcounseling/

Safe and Drug-Free Schools Program - www.ed.gov/offices/OESE/SDFS

Character Counts! – www.charactercounts.org

ResilienceNet - www.resilnet.uiuc.edu/

Made in the USA
Lexington, KY
27 March 2012